Selling Up!

How to Sell a Home for More Money and in Less Time

Gain a No-Nonsense Understanding of
the Good, the Bad, and the Ugly from a Pro

by
Nancie Balun
MFA, SFR®, ABR®
REALTOR®

Selling Up!
How to Sell a Home for More Money and Less Time

Published by: Nancie Balun, Bedminster, NJ 07921.
NBalun@optonline.net

All photographs were taken by the author to demonstrate lifestyle staging and photography techniques. Actual sellers' furniture and accessories were utilized.

Printed in the United States of America.

Dedication

I dedicate this book to my parents, husband, son, friends and clients who have always appreciated and supported my love of real estate. I dedicate this book to all sellers, real estate agents, builders, remodelers and investors committed to attaining and maintaining a positive attitude during the home selling process.

Big thanks to Art Wells, builder extraordinaire, who launched my career in new construction. Big thanks to Harold (Hal) Maxwell, President of Coldwell Banker Residential Brokerage of New Jersey and Rockland County, New York, for all his support over the last ten years. Big thanks to Robert Dusa and Brian Friedman for all their outstanding editing. To my editor/designer Karen Accavallo—thank you!

Table of Contents

A Personal Note from the Author

Sellers, real estate professionals, builders and investors deserve to know a better way to sell homes in the 21st Century. By sharing my 40 years of experiences in the promotion of real estate, discover why these "selling up" strategies and personal stories can provide a competitive advantage in the ever-changing dynamics of the real estate industry. Even if your home is in a "market depressed" community, make it ready for the upturn!

Robert Frost's poem, "The Road Not Taken," encapsulates my personal philosophy. I see the road, the neighborhood and the town. I then move forward with the best possible way to get a home sold quicker and for more money: beat the competition by choosing creative, stylish, self-assured, intelligent and innovative "less traveled" ideas.

Tired of hearing the age-old real estate solution: "drop the price?" Hear my new real estate truism: it's the house that sells the house. Let's get started!

Introduction

It has taken me 40 years to accumulate the skill set, experiences and knowledge to write this book, having bared witness to three tumultuous real estate crashes, since the early 1980s. My life-long connection with real estate began as the daughter of an electrical contractor during the 1950s. By the mid-1970s, advanced degrees from college provided me the opportunity to study art and architectural history and to develop keen marketing skills.

At the ripe old age of 25, the start of the 1980s "Golden Age of Building" provided an opportunity to begin my career in new home construction. Over the next 30 years my marketing skills stayed honed thanks to work with highly successful entrepreneurs who appreciated innovative ideas. It facilitated my standing as an award-winning new home marketing specialist, and, later after the birth of my son, an award-winning real estate journalist.

With the 2008 Great Recession, my new home selling and marketing skills were transferred to the resale market as a Sales Associate and five years later as a Broker Sales Associate. I quickly discovered sellers and listing agents were incorrectly, through no fault of their own, addressing the wrong problems.

After spending more than half of my life speaking before thousands of people as a housing consultant or writing as a journalist for my various columns, including "Ask Nancie," it's no secret that selling a home remains challenging and complicated.

It doesn't have to be! While reading each chapter, discover that maybe, just maybe, you have been asking the wrong questions AND speaking the wrong narratives about your home or listing. My strategies for selling a home for more money and in less time work—even in a sluggish real estate environment. It should make the home selling procedure more enjoyable, and hopefully less traumatic, especially when seeing so many more potential buyers coming to preview your home. Life is stressful enough; why shouldn't the process of selling a home be more gratifying?

My informal writing style includes quick and easy facts as well as some very popular but lesser known "Selling Up Tips" throughout the chapters. My personal stories and guidance stay uncomplicated, honest and totally unapologetic! Enjoy!

1

The Best Time to Sell a Home

Selling is Cyclical—determine the best season! By selling at the right time of the year, a home can sell faster and for more money. Are you ready for football—football?

Read on...

The spring market is the best time to sell, as more buyers are searching for the perfect home at this time of year. Amazingly, the spring market unofficially begins after the Super Bowl, sometime at the end of January or early February, which is actually late winter.

Why is that? There is no hard research on the observable fact, but the real estate industry has long understood that Americans love watching football especially on Sundays leading up to the Super Bowl. For example, ask any wife whose husband's love of football keeps him glued to the TV instead of going to look for a new place to live. That's not to say you won't find home buyers and sellers in spite of football (or even inclement weather), it's just the reality of the housing industry. By checking on-line real estate home listing sources like REALTOR.com, Trulia, Zillow and Multiple Listing sites, data can be extracted to determine which weeks of a month sell more homes during your spring market.

 Need to sell during football season? Stage a gathering room for a gaming party with snacks, footballs and video games during an open house.

Is Your Home Ready for the Holidays?

The holidays remain the worst time to sell for the simple reason people are busy preparing for them. During the winter holidays from November through January expect to see seasoned investors and bargain hunters who know this is the best time to buy. Sellers who need to sell during the holidays can often capitalize on those buyers who really need a home, and the fact that there are usually fewer homes (due to lower inventory) on the market during holiday times.

 Selling a home tastefully decorated in a Christ-mas theme with a big, beautifully decorated tree, festive garland, the smell of ginger cook-ies and a crackling fireplace can help elicit these favorite words: "Oh honey, we have to buy this house; it's the perfect home for the holidays!"

School's Out!

Don't forget: even if children are not part of your family, selling a home revolves around the school and college calendars. While there are plenty of single women looking to purchase, never assume the target market is only a single person who doesn't care about the school cycle. How do you know this single person may not be divorced and with a child? This is why the spring market rules. Parents want to close in time so they can move, unpack, decorate and be ready for the start of school.

 Consider adding to the family room/bedroom a variety of books, video games and toys for kids in the target market.

Vacation Time!

It's no secret Europeans take twice as many vacation days as Americans, and when the economy turns down, Americans take even fewer vacations. If a home is in a vacation destination or a home that people want to buy as a vacation or second home, expect these buyers during traditional vacation times such as President's week, spring break, Hanukah as well as during spring market. For those homes not in a vacation destination, July and August remain the least desirable time to sell because vacation time generally peaks during these months. Why? It happens right before students go back to school and college.

Create an exciting lifestyle theme to a vacation home. For example, add vintage skis, skates and snow shoes to a home near a ski resort.

If a vacation home is not being appraised correctly and preventing the buyer from securing a mortgage, consider an income analysis appraisal, if there is a profitable rental history for the property.

Get the Basics Done First!

To sell faster and for more money, a home must appeal to the greatest common denominator. A home should be continually updated while living in it, because it's impossible to predict if and when the day may arrive and you need to sell quickly. Additionally, by staggering updates to a home, it doesn't make the entire house look dated. Isn't a home one of the biggest investments and don't you deserve the utmost return? And don't forget the best reason for homeownership; to enjoy the finest quality of life that only an aesthetically pleasing home can provide.

Living with dirty, ugly carpeting? Get rid of it. No guarantee the new buyers will like a new (neutral-colored is best) carpet or if it will net a return on the improvement. One thing is for sure, worn carpeting is a buyer turn-off.

So consider selling a home when it's the best it can be by starting with these basic steps:

• Create a good first impression through curb appeal. Have a clean and well-maintained exterior. Spruce up the grass, shrubs and flower beds. Make the front door and entrance area appealing.

• Have a clean and well-maintained interior; ensure the foyer area looks attractive.

• De-clutter and organize your possessions, including closets, basement, garage and attic.

• Make potential buyers feel like it could be their home by removing an over-abundance of personal pictures, too taste-specific colors on the walls and excessive furniture and accessories in the rooms.

• Paint the walls neutral colors and use a satin finish that is washable. Don't use high gloss on the walls and ceilings, as it shows imperfections.

- Replace lights that are broken and uninteresting.

- Spruce up all cabinets in kitchen and bathrooms and interior and exterior doors; consider new hardware, if needed.

- The kitchen and master bedroom remain the two most important rooms in a home; it's critical that they look good.

- Make sure all the extra details are checked, such as attic, windows and doors, garage door(s), roof, siding, gutters, deck, patio and any other important features to your home.

- Ensure good working order of all mechanical items such as appliances, heating, ventilation and air conditioning (HVAC), septic system and well water.

A home should smell nice, especially when it's being shown to potential buyers. Entering a home with strong smells, especially of garlic, curry or fish, can be an unpleasant experience for many buyers. Sweet smells of cookies or mildly fragrant candles elicit a much more positive response to a home

2

It's Okay to be a Picky Seller

If you don't find the best possible real estate agent to sell a home, it becomes much harder to sell it faster and for more money. Reduce the stress of selling by reading some of my best and worst picks.

A Seller Should Not Sell Their Own Home!

I repeat, don't sell your own home unless you're licensed to sell real estate. I always discourage homeowners, builders and investors from selling their own home. According to national statistics, roughly 90% of buyers use an agent to help them find a home. If you're not working with an agent, can you see why 90% of agents with their buyers will not want to view/see your home? Worse yet, they may not even know it is for sale! Simply explained: buyers don't have to pay a real estate agent to show them homes for sale; it's free! Real estate commissions are paid by the seller. Why are most real estate agents not interested in showing your FSBO (for sale by owner) home? FSBO listings generally lack professionalism. Let's be honest: if it's difficult for professional sales associates to sell homes, what makes inexperienced sellers think they have the skillset to sell their own homes and can get as much exposure to the many online real estate marketing tools?

Generally speaking, people try to sell their own home because they either can't find a good professional real estate agent or they think if they don't pay a commission they will make more money. Oh my! Real estate professionals bring so many skills, including pricing and home preparation knowledge, absorption rates and other real estate statistical data to the selling of a home which sellers would have a difficult time duplicating on their own. Additionally, national data on selling prices shows real estate agents generally sell homes for more money. To learn more about selling statistics, go to the National Association of REALTORS® (NAR), the largest trade association, at REALTOR.com.

Selling Is a Team Effort

Selling a home involves a variety of people, including but not limited to sellers, buyers, real estate professionals, bankers, appraisers, home inspectors, title companies and lawyers. Your team should include the contractors needed in order to prepare a home for sale. Another member of the team should be a good real estate lawyer or title company. Note: Some states only require a title company to prepare a closing. The other member should be a real estate agent/associate, REALTOR®, broker/associate or broker. And it's possible; you may need to add an appraiser to the team if it's not possible to determine market value through a real estate agent's traditional resources. You may also need to add a consultant if your agent can't help with decluttering and beautifying your home in order to sell faster and for more money.

Real Estate Agent vs. REALTOR®; Broker Sales Associate vs. Broker

Know the difference between all of the above; it can make the process less stressful when trying to find the best in your local market. A real estate agent or associate took their required real estate classes, passed the state exam, and are working for a broker. A REALTOR® is also a real estate agent or associate but is a member of the National Association of REALTORS® and must abide by its standards and code of ethics. A broker associate has advanced studies and many more years of work experience and passed the state's broker exam but elected to work in a sales capacity. Only a broker can have other agents working for them and may also elect to list properties.

New Home Agent vs. Resale Agent

Since I began my career in new construction, I'm not trying to be biased; I'm trying to be plainspoken. A real estate agent who understands remodeling and construction can potentially bring more to the resale selling process. Why? If selling new construction, chances are the agent knows the cost of building a home, the latest buyer trends and the latest home products and services in the marketplace. That agent is probably better equipped at making a home more marketability through stylish improvements, such as furniture placement and lifestyle amenities, as well as marketing materials. New construction may continue to dwindle due in part to more limited land availability. This makes it more difficult for builders and sellers to find agents trained in advanced marketing capabilities which the study of new construction brings to the selling process. Sadly, classes in remodeling, construction and appraisal remain in short supply.

As a real estate professional, question why today's training in real estate does not include a standardized class that all real estate professionals must take in order to learn how a home is built or remodeled? Then again, car salespeople are not required to learn how a car is built or remodeled. That's just not right! Can anyone easily find a class on how to evaluate the cost of a garage or kitchen or the knowledge one needs to help price up one home from another? Advocate for the advancement of basic building and construction training in order to raise the bar of our profession and to better serve today's sellers and buyers. Go to the National Association of Builders (NAHB) at www.NAHB.org to learn more about buyer and seller trends as well as educational classes on the basics of new construction.

Buying a new home remains popular, but finding new construction is far more limited than years past. Why not make your home look newer and beautified like a model home? By doing so, it broadens your home's appeal to the greatest common denominator.

My House of Worship Member vs. a Stranger From a Reputable Real Estate Office in Town

Should I trust a real estate agent who is a member of my house of worship to sell my home? He or she must be honest and trustworthy, right? While trustworthiness and honesty are paramount, if a friend from your church/synagogue/mosque/temple can't help with beautiful photography, any decluttering/staging issues, and identifying what is appealing and unappealing to your targeted buyers, why settle for less? Consider visiting a reputable real estate office in your town and asking for a referral from the office manager.

A Good Friend vs. Family Member

Use a good friend or family friend as long as this professional sales agent knows your targeted buyers, your town, and how to effectively market and sell your home. It can be a lot more comfortable to work with family or a good friend. But on the flip side, if things don't go well with the sale, it may be tougher to scold a friend or family member. If you decide your good friend or family member may be too removed from your area, ask to refer a sales associate through their company's referral network.

Don't be intimated by anyone! Play it safe and check out potential agents on real estate sites like Trulia and Zillow or an agent's personal web site. Read client reviews and testimonials to ensure you find the best agent to sell your home.

Men vs. Women

I don't know why this is, and I have found no scientific evidence to confirm this. I just know that I see this father complex more than I can tell you. Why do sellers seem more inclined to believe an older gentleman is better at listing homes? Is it because the man reminds them of a father or grandfather figure? Why do sellers believe this charming older gentleman with a kind yet strong voice brings greater value? A house may need decluttering and furniture placement and lots of marketing needs. Surely, he must be able to sell the home? Think again! Generally speaking, I'm just not sure if it's in most men's nature to be able to intelligently discuss ideas about wallpaper; paint colors and furniture placement, especially if needed. Now that I have said this, I don't want to make anyone mad. There are lots of great and talented male sales associates who can sell up; it's a question of finding them. According to the National Association of REALTORS®, 42% of today's REALTORS® are male. 58% of today's REALTORS® are female and the median age is 57.

Today, sales agents typically use mortgage advisors often affiliated with their brokerage company in order to get their clients' pre-approval for a mortgage. Gone are the days of having a real estate agent qualifying clients. Agents should be showing the home after their client receives a pre-approval letter from the lender indicating how much can be borrowed.

The Top Producer Myth Dispelled

Experience counts, but don't rule out an experienced real estate agent with fewer clients but lots more know-how and abundantly more time for a home's listing. Not all great agents desire to remain "top producers" (informally defined as high dollar volume sales associates). In addition, never take for granted a top producer has the skill set needed to sell your home. Top producers prefer to be money driven not service driven. I have met many top producers who prefer to do their business the "sell down" (old school) approach, because they lack the time or desire. Let's be honest, it takes a lot more time to work with sellers who need lots of help with their home in order to sell up. It is far quicker and easier to sell your home just the way you have it (old and flamboyant wallpaper and all)! It's far easier to not do a thorough market assessment and just overprice it. It's far easier to drop the price of the home, if unable to get it sold, rather than determine why the potential buyers didn't like it.

There are plenty of old school and poorly trained real estate professionals with or without a great following that take a listing and suggest no improvements (even though the red paint in the living room is hideous), overprice it to get the listing, and then drop the price in order to sell.

Each time a home is shown, collect positive and negative feedback from the agents and clients. Use this data constructively and wisely.

3

Easy, Cheesy, Tricks of the Trade to Avoid

We've all heard those quick-selling pitches over the years; here are my top picks.

You Can Get Me How Much Money for My House?

Never, ever be so trusting to think that any real estate agent can get more money than the real estate marketplace dictates. Don't select an agent because he or she quoted the highest listing price for the home than any other sales associate. No one has a crystal ball, and no one can predict the final sale price of a home! Note: during a housing downturn, even my guidance may not work. If there are no buyers in the market; there are no buyers in the market. Additionally, if lenders don't want to lend money to potential buyers in the neighborhood or don't want to properly appraise a home's true value due to too many short sales in your neighborhood, it becomes very difficult to sell a home.

As a seller, it is your job to agree to a selling price. It is the seller who must finalize the listing price, not the agent. Conversely, the listing agent should be presenting comparable properties that include sold and unsold homes in your area and suggest a list price based on the facts of the marketplace.

You Can Drop the Commission?

Remember the old adage; you get what you pay for. Well, it remains true in the housing industry. If someone is willing to drop their commission below the local or regional average or works for a discount brokerage firm, is it wise to think that agent can provide high quality services compared to a full-service brokerage firm? Sellers who live in more distressed areas are even more susceptible to "boutique" (small, independent) brokerage companies who try to stay competitive by often making big promises they usually can't keep. Sellers beware of short-cut selling!

I Didn't Know My House Looks Better In Pictures?

If an agent takes a picture with a wide angle camera lens and the room doesn't look that big, don't you think potential buyers will be underwhelmed when they walk into your home and see a smaller-looking room? No one wants to come to a home and see rooms that are smaller than the pictures shown on the Internet. Potential buyers like to see a home surrounded by beautiful trees but get very upset when they arrive to see your home and discover the trees never existed. Avoid photographs or an artist's rendering that exaggerates the truth about your home!

Create a focal point in each room you photograph. Try to use natural lighting in the photograph, because a naturally light or sunny room elicits a more positive response. Night photography of your home's exterior is great, if there is nice landscape lighting to accent the home's architecture. 3-D Matterport photography is growing in popularity. Drone photography, to capture aerial views of a home, is growing in popularity and is a great way to display a home with interesting roof lines or large acreage.

It's Snowing In the Spring?

If a picture of the exterior to the home has snow all around and it's during spring or summer; update the image. Always freshen up a listing with the latest pictures of the way the home looks both outside and inside throughout the seasons. For those who live in states with few seasonal changes, aren't you the lucky ones!

Do include in the listing seasonal pictures of the home and/or the surrounding area, if you think it will add value and explain the year-round beauty of living in the home.

You Have A Buyer for My Home?

We have all heard this story, whether a seller or agent. Why are some sales people notoriously known for saying or doing anything to get a listing, especially if the bread-winner of their home and desperate to bring home the "bacon." Never, ever lie! It's unethical and lowers our professional standing and it makes sellers very angry. Sales agents who are members of the National Association of REALTOR®s, be sure to flaunt it. NAR members are required to live by the Golden Rule and a Code of Ethics and are required to take an ethics class every two years.

If I Make These Improvements, I Will Get My Money Back?

A good agent, who understands construction and remodeling costs, as mentioned earlier, should know that replacing an old unstylish kitchen before selling is no guarantee to a return on that investment. Making improvements at the time of selling is never the best time. To learn which improvements net the greatest return in your area, try home improvement sites like Houzz.com.

Get to know the latest design trends, visit on-line blogs and design sites, including HGTV and DIY.

Your House Is Perfect; You Don't Need To Do A Thing!

If a home is nowhere near PERFECT, a light bulb should go off in your head. Any agent who says a home is perfect (when it's not) is probably unwilling or unsure of how to talk about the help the home needs in order to sell it faster and for more money. If it's impossible to find an agent in your area that is good at selling, consider a new strategy. Hire a professional sales agent and a home stager (designer/merchandiser/artist that specializes in presenting rooms in a home) or marketing/housing consultant to work with all of you. Try using the professional connection site LinkedIn to help in the search.

Sales agents are often afraid to tell a seller how bad the home might look for fear of being rejected for the listing. Selling a home requires not thinking like a homeowner but rather to think like a savvy business person. Don't take unflattering comments about a home personally; it is constructive criticism—use it wisely!

4

Understanding the Mindset of Buyers

Sooo....celebrating the symbiotic relationship between the sellers and a hand-picked listing agent. Excellent! Now, it's time to keep an open mind and focus on the most critical component of the "selling up" process. Before marketing a home for sale, seller and agent need to collectively project who will be the targeted buyers. If you think the home is perfect for a family or single person, it is no longer enough to think in those guileless qualifying terms. Carefully explore the following buyer types, and, while doing so, try to postulate who the potential buyers might be and how they might react when seeing the home for the first time. Will they say, "Oh honey, I love this home!" Or, will they make a quick exit for the front door after a five minute tour!

The HGTV Buyer

Welcome to the world of HGTV (Home & Garden Television), an American basic cable and satellite television channel. Before the cable industry introduced a plethora of reality shows (over two decades ago), answers to questions about how to fix and decorate or how to sell and buy a home could be found primarily in magazines and books. It proved commonplace for buyers to purchase a home that lacked charisma. Those days passed! To sell a home without proper planning often leads to poor performance!

Millions of viewers watch HGTV every day to enjoy the buzz of trading up, re-investing, and the buying and selling of the American Dream! HGTV buyers love seeing a smartly outfitted home. And, viewers think redoing or flipping an ugly home must be easy to do. To prevent these buyers from passing on the home, consider making it HGTV ready or if not possible, just keep the home looking awful but price it cheap for an investor to buy!

Let me give a simple example of what it can mean to be "HGTV ready." Let's just say the sellers are a nice retiring couple living in a vintage mid-century (1950's), ranch-style home. They refurbished the original cabinets, bathrooms and fireplace, but, in early 2000 desired beige Berber carpets, and never replaced them. Maybe mid-century architecture is beloved by younger buyers in their late 30's in your area. If economically feasible, consider removing that carpet with stylish wooden floors of the period. If not economically feasible, consider placing some 1950-inspired shag area rugs over the Berber in order to attract these younger and trendier buyers.

Double Income Trouble

Before the age of a two-income family, mom stayed home to raise her family and gussie up the family abode. She devoted lots more time around the house. Current government reports indicate almost two-thirds of families continue to be maintained by two working parents. Today, divorced, married, married with kids, first-time home buyers and move-up buyers continue to work longer hours and simply don't have the time to fix up a home. Or, they don't have the skillset to fix up a home. Some in the media say we are bearing witness to a "low-maintenance movement" with many of today's buyers.

Buyers prefer to understand the many costs to homeownership. Consider including in your marketing materials some of the following data: cost for average utility bills per month, rate of rise in Homeowner Association dues, and replacement costs of big ticket items, such as roof and furnace.

The Millennials: Born From Baby Boomers or Generation X

The millennials cometh! Hoping to buy or rent their first place. Born from the early 1980s to the early 2000s, they now outnumber the Baby Boomers. They may carry sizeable college debt. They often witnessed their parents' home values plummet. Be prepared; it may cause them to feel less confident about the home buying process. They gravitate to cities so they can live closer to work. They really don't desire to commute in a car or train for hours or to want a large home in the burbs, at least not for right now. During their middle and high school years, millennials may not have learned many skills through the use of their hands. It proved not uncommon for woodworking, trade schools and hands-on learning classes to be reduced or eliminated. Additionally, many dual income parents did not have the time to pass along basic carpentry, electrical and plumbing skills. Luckily, millennials maintain constant and immediate access to the Internet to find answers, including one of their least favorite problems: how to stop and fix an overflowing toilet. Aww! They want things updated and set up with any technology to make living in their home more convenient. They may ask a lot of questions about the home buying process. Make sure to share lots of detailed information about the home in the marketing campaign. Leave every manual related to any and everything being sold with the home.

If it's possible to store every manual for your home electronically, millennials will feel right at home and that much faster! Include in the marketing materials mortgage data, especially what it would cost to live in the home versus renting.

The Helicopter Parents

There's another obstacle in the buying and selling of homes—helicopter parents: hovering around their millennial children, while searching for a first home to fit their lifestyle and location. According to Wikipedia, helicopter parents hover overhead, helping their child whether needed or not, also known as over-parenting. Over the past 40 years, I laid bystander to many a parent helping a first-time home buyer both financially and emotionally. I am devoting more time to explaining this phenomenon, because it's difficult to sell a home for more money and faster if it's not possible to determine the real decision makers.

Admittedly, good reasons for parental involvement easily come to mind. The first obvious reason: most parents want to ensure their kids follow a sound investment model and fully understand the cost to update or repair a home. The second reason: if parents contribute money to the purchase, they want to ensure a return on their investment. And lastly, some parents play a bigger role in family lives than others.

Not all parents act with love and support, while their children house hunt and ultimately make a home selection. Some can behave very badly. Why do parents step over the line when their children decide to buy their first home? What can the first-time home buyer do when their parents interfere in the process? I don't think trying to come between parents and children works well, especially when they may be contributing to the purchase and evoke parental privileges.

Undoubtedly, some parents will try too hard to persuade their children to listen to them. Some parents do it because they feel they don't trust or like their children's opinion of a house. Some parents can be too competitive with their kids or unhappy with themselves or carrying emotional issues that can cause them to act irresponsibly and ultimately cause the children not to buy a home. Since most parents would find it difficult to explain why they prefer to do this, let's leave it to the sociologists and economists to gather those statistics.

In many instances the younger generation doesn't necessarily think about a home in the same way as their parents. For example, first-time home buyers often prefer the convenience of a house near a train station or on a busy main street so they can walk to public transportation. I have seen first timers prefer more unusual architectural styles over classic, mainstream architecture in their region of the country. I have also seen young buyers prefer to live near a major highway and listen to traffic noise to the chagrin of their parents, because homes near highway noise typically sell for less, but can create a more convenient commute.

So what can be done to help parents and children during the home buying process? Life is filled with risks; give adult children the confidence to learn the skills needed to buy wisely through guidance, not dictatorship.

An agent must sell and then resell each family member who walks through the door of the home when working with helicopter parents.

Generation X

Demographers tend to use birth dates ranging from the early 1960s to the early 1980s when determining Generation X, the oldest being in their mid-fifties. This means they may be looking for homes in 55 plus communities. They possess great earning potential. Many remain committed to raising a family of school-aged children and value work-life balance. They won't necessarily gravitate to the city, especially with children; they look for towns with good schools. Some may need a home to include aging parents. Home buying and selling is not new to them. They understand the possibility of job losses. The mortgage process doesn't intimidate them, and they know it's wise to plan for a rainy day by securing a secondary loan on their home.

Gen X continues to look for healthy lifestyle conveniences. Consider this subliminal impression: play up healthy eating by displaying a few cook books. Consider a cook book boasting the ever popular Mediterranean diet.

The Baby Boomers

The Baby Boomers have been downsizing for some time. Born between 1946 and 1964, this generation really excelled at moving to the suburbs for the big house and often longer commute. But now, many empty-nesters over the age of 55 continue to move out of their older homes to discover a whole new way of life. Empowered with years of experience in home ownership and a keen sense of what they need in their retirement home, these wiser and more practical buyers continue to search for their perfect resale or new home. According to the National Association of Home Builders, they don't all want to retire by a pool or golf course but, instead, want to return to a big city.

A survey compiled by Merrill Lynch reveals boomers don't necessarily want their parents' version of retirement. And why would they? According to the study, the majority of boomers plan to keep working and earning in retirement, but they will do this by "cycling" between periods of work and leisure to create an entirely new "model of retirement." 76 percent plan to "retire" from their current job or career at around age 64 and then launch into an entirely new endeavor. And as a result of living longer, boomers believe they will be "younger" by working longer.

After analyzing these results, Merrill Lynch took the study and cleverly created and identified five distinctly different types of retiring baby boomers: "empowered trailblazers," "wealth-builders," "leisure lifers," "anxious idealists" and "stretched and stressed."

What else do baby boomers like? Elevators! Elevators continue to take up residence at active adult communities. Not long ago active adult housing dictated the cute ranch-style home neighborhoods or the upscale two-level home community. But with land more difficult and more expensive to acquire in some parts of the country, and active adults desirous of living near their former residences, the creation of mid-rise and high-rise housing continues to increase in popularity.

Let your agent know it's okay to clean or fix things during any house showings. Stuff happens! For example, sellers can forget to remove shaving hairs in the bathroom sink, to make a bed or correct a tilted lamp shade or perhaps return a misplaced chair. Don't make a seller feel guilty; calmly address the issue for a house showing.

The Greatest Generation

The Greatest Generation continues to sustain dwindling numbers. Don't be surprised if their homes appear outdated and filled with lots of antiques, collectibles and memorabilia. However, don't be too quick to renovate before asking this question: quality vintage vs. cheap remodel. For example, a vintage home with a classy 50-year-old bathroom or kitchen in impartial colors, such as beige, gray or white, may be considered stylish. Research the home and town before jumping into costly changes that may not net a return on the investment.

Some buyers remain especially interested in nicely renovated homes owned by seniors who elected to age-in-place, especially those who sustained decreased mobility. They may have added a chair lift, enlarged doorways and bathrooms, or made the kitchens safer by lowering the countertops.

5

Beyond the Basic Buyer Type

As a home gets shown to more and more potential buyers, don't be surprised if the projected "ideal" buyers evolve and change. While identifying buyer types, consider if the list price for the home is consistent with their potential financial profile. Does the home price make the most sense based on the number of projected buyers in the marketplace, comparable home prices and the amenities and features within the neighborhood and community as a whole? Here are some additional profiles of buyers typically encountered during the selling of a home.

The Bargain Hunters and the Empty House of the Transferee

When the economy soars higher, companies may be more willing to pay for a transferee's move. Sometimes the employee moves out for the transfer before the sale of the home. Sometimes they settle for a buyout package; the company buys the home (so the new employee can purchase their next home for this new job) and the company must sell the vacant home. Whether the owner or company has to sell, a house without furniture looks uninviting and impersonal to most potential buyers. To the bargain hunters, who live for the next big giveaway, it means there is an opportunity to try and purchase the house for a deep discount. When it appears that a home looks as if no one cares about it anymore—buyers see it as devoid of life and a lifestyle!!

To sell faster and earn more money, try virtual staging (photography technology that can make a room look fully-furnished) or photograph each room before taking everything away. Remember: showing a furnished home in pictures is better than showing it vacant. However, fewer potential buyers can walk into an empty kitchen or bathroom and feel a real emotional attachment after seeing pictures of what it could look like. You won't hear, "oh honey, this is such a homey kitchen," or "what a romantic bathroom," when walking into empty rooms.

 Think room vignettes! The kitchen and master suite remain THE top rooms for buyers. If possible, display a table and chair set for the dining area. Place artwork where needed to make a vignette warm and inviting. Accessorize the kitchen countertops with real-life items, such as a cookbook and bottle of wine with glasses. Accessorize each bathroom with towels, decorative soaps and neutral fabric treatments for any shower and window. Place a rug and artwork in the foyer. Display empty, high-end department stores' bags and shoe boxes in the closets.

The Planned Community Dwellers

Across America, professionally and often elaborately planned clubhouses for both large and small communities continue to advance social and recreational activities. Many buyers realize that home ownership means more than simply buying a home. Planned communities include a plethora of amenities, such as swimming and wading pools, tennis and basketball courts, playgrounds, exercise gyms, whirlpool tubs, security measures, walking paths and golf courses. Some planned communities are age-restricted but many remain open to all, especially to buyers who may want to enjoy swinging a golf club, swimming laps, hitting a few balls, stretching at yoga, strolling down a sidewalk or soaring to the sky in a swing. Clubhouse communities allow residents to gather for business or socialize with friends in a beautiful setting not far from their home. Show potential buyers how much fun it is to enjoy the lifestyle of the community. Community-style living with a clubhouse and recreational facilities built into the neighborhood remains a great selling point! These communities promote an active lifestyle that revolves around exercising and leisurely activities.

Use photographs of all the amenities within the planned community in the marketing campaign. Don't forget to include any newsletters and any information that helps potential buyers see the value of living in a planned community.

The Green Buyer

We all know why it's important to conserve our natural energy; it's the American way! Builders, remodelers, buyers and everyone in between knows that it is the right thing to do for our environment. But how well are we doing, and can we be doing more? Energy is front page news every day, and whether it's prices at the pump or getting shocked when opening a utility bill, consumers are becoming more concerned with their energy usage, or more appropriately, their energy costs.

Many more buyers understand the significance of saving our natural resources, especially those that are not renewable. They gravitate to homes designed around today's Green Movement in order to save money, help the environment, and live a healthier lifestyle. The Tiny House popularity reflects the desire for a smaller footprint on our planet through technology and efficient living concepts. Electronically wired homes or Smart Homes help save energy, too. Green buyers appreciate stylish recycling areas, composting stations and pesticide-free gardens. They also appreciate concrete products, zinc countertops, stainless steel and soapstone. Water-saving plumbing products and energy-efficient lighting, appliances and HVAC should be highlighted in the marketing materials to ensure showing how a home can save money and energy whether a green buyer or not.

To learn more about the many green initiatives and to better understand how to build a more earth-friendly home, the National Association of Home Builders developed a course entitled "Green Building for Building Professionals." Those who wish to learn about this ever-expanding movement can go to www.NAHB.org.

Own a hybrid car? Display during open house. Own an electric vehicle support system? Describe in marketing literature.

Do You Feng Shui?

Don't know a thing about Feng Shui? Chances seem high that the home isn't Feng Shui ready. Many potential buyers believe in this ancient Chinese art of ideal living conditions for a more fun and happier home. For example, positive energy can be stimulated through water features, plants and flowers, paint colors and furniture placement. Those following Feng Shui arrange a home according to its principles in order to enhance their health, wealth and wisdom. To learn more, consider taking a class or buy one of the many books on this fascinating ancient art in order to appeal to the Feng Shui way of life buyers.

Don't overlook any potential buyer who may deeply believe in Feng Shui. Display a Feng Shui book and consider adding a few simple principles, such as a correctly placed wind chime.

Let's Bark and Meow for our Animal Lovers

One crusade seems destined to grow stronger in our country: the pet movement. If skeptical, just check out the ever-growing hotels that cater to owners with pets, the myriad of carrying cases for pets, and the restaurants designed just for pets and their owners.

Conversely, some planned communities restrict any kind of pet in anyone's home. Townhouse and condominium communities seem determined to keep pets out after decades of Homeowner Association battles as a result of, most notably, the continuous barking dog noises and piling up of feces across a community's landscape.

Don't be surprised if buyers gravitate to homes for some of the animal love provided by sellers who cater to animals. Dogs, cats, pigs, horses and more can be found housed in some rather fancy digs. Barns, stables, dog rooms, cat rooms and the like continue to grow in demand. If enjoying the lifestyle afforded with the high maintenance and expense of being an animal owner, be sure to showcase the home's animal love.

If extra space is available, consider a dog or cat room (perhaps near the laundry room) designed with pet art, bedding and toys.

Adventure Seekers

Fresh air, sunny meadows, rustic settings and wildlife seem to be in more abundance when buying a home away from the city or suburbs. Buyers who crave to be in the countryside enjoy an active lifestyle filled with the wonderful sights and sounds of nature. So sell up the many local recreational activities from rolling hills and nature trail walks to bridle trails, fishing and hunting. Don't forget those who prefer farmlands and ponds and still others who want to be near a lake or the ocean for boating and fishing. And finally, sell the home's appeal if it includes leisurely pursuits from antique shopping and wine tasting to hay wagon rides and picking of fruits at nearby farms.

Buyers care about their health, especially when seeking homes near nature. Play some relaxing "sounds of nature" music during the home's showing to connote a relaxing home environment.

The Affordable Home Buyers

Unfortunately, buyers in less desirable, distressed areas of a state or low income communities and towns rarely get the "cream of the crop" sales agents and brokers. Sales agents simply do not want to work where they believe crimes may occur. It takes the same amount of work to list and sell a $600,000 home as it does a $70,000 home. Thankfully, this book can help with the process. Affordable housing buyers expect to see nice things in a nice-looking home, just like anyone else.

 Give potential buyers that "champagne" look on their "beer" budget! Generally speaking, people want what they can't have. Some even go into homes way over budget just to fantasize about what life could be like if they owned a home out of their price range. Consider placing some high-end department stores' paper shopping bags in the closets. It connotes a sense that you know how to pamper yourself. It also makes the buyer think that if you shop for luxury items, you must shop for nice things attached to the home.

The Luxury Home Buyers

Much has been written about the lifestyle of the upscale homebuyers. Everyone assumes a luxury home must look luxurious. Not always true, especially if the home hasn't been updated in 20 years or more and the owners didn't install timeless, classic features. If the drapes look tired and dirty, take them down. Remove any trendy floor tile of fads gone by. Take away very personalized art, such as a gold swan faucet in the master bathroom or a dragon sculpture on the front lawn.

Good taste doesn't come as a guarantee even if it's possible to afford a luxury home. No longer have the means to remove ugly, dated features in the home? Highlight the best of what is there, such as beautifully detailed mahogany or cherry cabinets, double staircases, nine to ten foot ceilings as well as any vaulted, coffer or barreled ceilings. Affluent buyers love thick, custom moldings, marble floors and stone fireplaces as well as outdoor pools, cabanas and tennis courts. Play up popular architectural details that include: half circle, full circle and transom windows, French doors, sliding barn doors, wooden wall paneling and built-in cabinets.

When showing a luxury home, add ambiance by lighting the fireplace, turning on the ceiling and wall lights, and uncovering a pool table. Have a sunroom or breakfast room designed with ceiling fans and tall windows that flood in light? Help potential buyers see how they can relax and enjoy their morning breakfast while taking in nature's views.

A buyer of higher means seeks spacious floor plans with rooms of all shapes, sizes and heights. Size, however, is not the only determining factor when defining the upscale home marketplace. While luxury remains heavily defined by big and spacious homes, luxury can be found in more efficient floor plans complicated to construct because of angled walls, expansive heights, intricate architectural details, extensive staircases and complex topography; those need to be highlighted, too.

Don't forget to showcase a home's increased value due to the cost of the many new home products and amenities installed over the years. Highlight rooms for explicit tasks and special times and those that fulfill the lifestyle of the luxury buyer, such as a music room, sun room, conservatory, maid's quarters, his-and-her bathrooms, wine cellar, home gym, art gallery and media room. These buyers like spaces that can serve more than one function. For example, a room that can be a home office or a playroom for younger children or a finished basement so children of any age can have additional playing space. Parents especially like this because it keeps the mess and noise contained. High-end buyers love kitchens with multiple dishwashers, expensive countertops and restaurant-quality appliances. They have discretionary income so they view cooking as a hobby and a pleasurable experience for invited guests. And finally, to prepare for these buyers' future lifestyle as seniors, a home designed with an elevator from the first to the second floor or a first floor bedroom can be a real plus!

If you have a luxury car, display it outside the garage during any showings. Set the dining room table as if you were having a dinner party.

6

What Do Buyers Really Want in Their Home?

When selling a home it's so important to ensure the following top five "wants" of buyers receive plenty of attention. While there certainly are many "wishes" buyers consider critical, these top five seem destined to remain most important for a successful home sale.

Number 1: Are You Kitchen-Worthy?

Our kitchen remains THE place to gather for eating, partying or simply paying our bills. And according to the National Kitchen & Bath Association (advocates for safety in the kitchen), here are some of the timeless ways they hope you will try to achieve it.

• Use proper lighting. Include good general lighting and task lighting and avoid lots of glare and shadows.

• Use slip-resistant flooring. Try using a matte-finish wood, textured wood vinyl plank or soft-glazed ceramic tile. If selecting tile, consider using a throw rug around wet areas for added precautions.

- Keep a fire extinguisher handy. Keep it visibly located near an exit door and according to your local fire department's code.

- Keep electrical switches, plugs and light fixtures away from water sources and wet hands. Building codes require ground-fault circuit interrupters near moisture areas.

- Regulate water temperatures and devices. Use anti-scald faucets or pressure-balanced valves that equalize the hot and cold water or faucets with pre-programmed temperature settings.

- Have a safe cooking surface. Make sure the burners are staggered or have one straight row to avoid being scalded by steam from boiling pots.

- Use the kitchen space safely. Consider traffic flow through the kitchen that keeps the cooking area free from traffic congestion, and consider using rounded edge countertops.

Kitchen-worthiness not only means focusing on safety but also focusing on the style of the cabinets, the type of materials used to make them, and the quality of their construction. The material used for cabinets continually changes in popularity. One year it could be red oak, another year it could be painted white and the list goes on to include maple, walnut, cherry and non-wood products. Cabinet styles change all the time too—from simple Shaker to furniture quality detailing. Glazes, paints and stain colors abound. It's hard to determine if any given buyers will love dark or light-colored cabinets—it's OK! But one thing is for sure, if it's not possible to spend money to update old cabinets, consider some inexpensive updates by making the hardware attractive and making the cabinets clean and polished in appearance. The key thing to remember: most buyers don't want to remodel the kitchen after buying a home. It's too costly, time consuming and stressful! So try your best to make it look as good as a budget allows.

Lighting should be aesthetically pleasing to the targeted buyers and installed at the proper height and size over an island, peninsula and/or table. Countertops need to be very appealing, since they play such a big role in food preparation. Laminate countertops and Corian continue to dwindle in popularity, mainly because they scratch so easily. Quartz continues to gain in popularity, given it's easier to maintain than granite and marble. Surprisingly, green buyers gravitate to the overly soft material found in soapstone and the super hard materials found in concrete for their countertops. And lastly, appliance colors and functionality can never be taken for granted. Buyers don't like spending money for new appliances. And let's not forget the never ending battle over the preference for gas vs. electric stoves and cooktops.

Generally speaking, one thing is for certain. Buyers appreciate those sellers who invest in their kitchen while living in their home, because it continues to be such a popular and enjoyable place to spend time. While the process of updating a kitchen, whether big or small, can be painful, the end result can be very satisfying to potential buyers. If living with high-quality wood cabinets in the kitchen but a really outdated countertop, consider adding a timeless countertop and backsplash in order to make the kitchen more stylish. Avoid costly and overly trendy tiles which may not appeal to as many buyers.

Buyers love to envision themselves cooking in a kitchen, but they do not love coming into a house that smells like fish, garlic or curry. Make sure the home always smells great during a showing. Consider using candles, sprays, incense or (the classic) desserts baking in the oven. Consider a central location for all the chargers you have for today's ever-evolving technology.

Number 2: Make a Big Splash in the Bath

Homeowners continue to have a love affair with bathrooms, particularly the master bathroom. For a long time, bathrooms remained basically the same conventional style, designed with a tub, sink and toilet—but not anymore. Master bathrooms keep growing in size. Two sinks in the main and master bathroom appear more commonplace. Powder rooms continue to evolve into something more than just a utilitarian space as we see them designed with pedestal sinks, ornate vanities, wood flooring and marble. An endless variety of sinks, cabinets and plumbing fixtures can be found along with elegant tile designs and colorful light fixtures.

Buyers appreciate when sellers put a lot of time and effort into the updating of bathrooms. That said; let me provide caution about using products those consumers know and identify from the local "do it yourself" stores. Try the Internet or local shops to see if it's possible to find more interesting and less common lights, flooring and cabinetry. Yes, it's smart to save money on home products but not smart when everyone knows it.

Buyers also appreciate a separate stall shower with multiple shower heads, a fancy tub and a private commode room. They enjoy seeing all kinds of lighting: lighted mirrors, recessed lights, formal chandeliers and informal decorative lighting. Buyers like other kinds of details, such as porcelain, marble, granite, stone, slate, wood tiles and limestone on the floor or walls, and as in the kitchen, moisture-resistant wood or non-wood cabinets.

Master bathrooms within the owner's suite have become as important as the kitchens of yesterday thanks in large part to two working partners. Homeowners today really value quiet time where they can relax after working a long, hard day. Bathrooms have become a necessary luxury instead of simply a place where they spend very little time. Buyers now want a room large enough to feel pampered after putting the day's stress behind them. Taking a nice hot bath or shower to unwind, before settling into bed in a room fit for royalty, can make homeowners feel ready for the next day's challenges.

Have a small bathroom? Try photographing and staging it with a romantic flare: burning candles, plush towels and spa bathrobe.

Number 3: Is There Fun in the Family Room?

Today's family rooms should be exciting yet functional gathering places whether in a single family home, town home or condominium. Who doesn't love the drama of two-story ceilings, stacks of windows, floor to ceiling fireplaces, and wall-to-wall doors? Old World charm remains a classic appeal so play up any ceilings higher than eight feet, wood paneled walls, built-in cabinets and thick moldings around the windows, doors and fireplaces. And don't forget, buyers love to live with the latest in home entertainment technology.

Buyers continue to enjoy the drama created by a raised or sunken family room, since it can visually separate the family room from an adjoining kitchen or dining area, while leaving the overall area open for interaction. However, not everyone appreciates an open family room and kitchen. Some don't like the smells of food easily traveling to other rooms, including fireplace smoke.

Family room design trends are also a function of who will live in the home. Families with small children usually prefer a family room open to the kitchen and/or breakfast room so the youngsters can be observed, especially while preparing meals. Families with teens usually prefer just the opposite, a family room completely or partially separated from the eating area. This allows each room to be used for different things at the same time, and it eliminates noise and smells that can more easily travel into open spaces. Others enjoy a family room designed with a pass-through or service bar between the kitchen and family room for informal munches. Some families want a second family room in the basement for the 'big toys', such as exercise equipment, pool table or extra-large TV. Some don't; the phone, tablet or computer, etc. is where they view/stream news, movies, etc.

And what do buyers prefer when they don't have or are no longer raising children? Buyers over the age of 55 typically prefer having no family or living room, but rather one big great room. These couples often prefer an open floor plan.

For buyers moving into their second or third home, a family room designed differently from the last house is usually desired, unless the family has children whose needs may dictate otherwise. As an example, many people who bought a home in the 80's, when open floor plans between the family room and kitchen were at their peak, often prefer their next home have more separation between the two rooms.

Whether it is big toys or equipment, buyers accumulate lots of things, besides furniture, to put into the busiest room in a home. Some buyers want a computer in the family room to accommodate the many computer games for children or for surfing the web. Other buyers envision their family room as an entertainment/media room. Family rooms that cater to a casual lifestyle continue to grow steadily in popularity... and show no signs of slowing down.

Set up an area in the family room, if possible, for displaying video games, board games and reading corner. By demonstrating how the room can be used for the targeted buyers, it will solicit more positive feedback about the home.

Number 4: Think About Storage and Flexible Spaces

Storage never falls out of style. Storage remains in demand whether inside the home, down in the basement, up in the attic, or outside the home, and from storage shed to pool cabana. Buyers will look more favorably upon the home if it incorporates a wide range of storage options. Buyers always have lots of things they want to store away. There are big toys for kids and adults, lots of food supplies and plenty of seasonal clothes, among others. And for pet owners, there is always a need for pet supply storage.

The biggest change in storage has occurred in the kitchen regardless of the home's price. Since recycling was introduced, many buyers want extra garbage space in the kitchen. Extra space for trash management, recycling and composting is also desired for the garage, laundry center or mud room.

With the introduction of discount stores that sell bulk food as well as home and office products, more storage areas are needed. Storage needs are also changing due to the increase in toys owned by parents and children. Many owners would love a third garage bay to accommodate today's ride-on cars/tractors, bicycles, motorcycles, golf carts, golf clubs and hockey equipment.

With the popularity of recreational vehicles, it has created a need to increase the height and width of the garage door. If the home has eight feet high doors instead of the standard seven feet height, flaunt them. If the garage was built without lolly columns between bays, and has a steel beam for structural support, it's a great way to show the extra space needed for pool equipment, patio furniture, garden equipment, power washer, wider vehicles and even small boats.

Every family has different storage needs, so show off any storage flex-space. They may include a workshop space and workbench in the garage, a basement finished to accommodate a playroom for tots, rec room for teens, workout area, pet space or a craft and hobby studio. With more Americans electing to do some work from a home office, showcase unwanted or underutilized space as an office.

A home designed with widespread storage to include guest closets, family closets, pantries and storage closets can really get potential buyers excited. So advertise those closets! Have first and second floor closets to accommodate two 20-foot long central vacuum hoses or seasonal item storage over the garage? How about an attic with an entrance door and retractable stairs? What about converted space under steps turned into closets, or cedar closets in the bedrooms or basement or a walk-in pantry in the kitchen?

Buyers, from active adults to move-up buyers, continue to be interested in living in their home devoid of clutter. Some even enjoy seeing an entire spare bedroom turned into a storage closet and having it professionally planned with built-in shelves, cabinets and shoe racks. Some sellers are taking rooms with vaulted ceilings and converting the second level space to storage.

Gone are the days of wood shelving that over time could warp. Wrapped wire and non-wood shelving are affordable and very popular. If the home has professionally designed storage in the garage, basement, or master bedroom walk-in closet, advertise this in the listing as it adds value to the home. And finally, consider enclosing space under a high deck by installing lattice in order to create storage for items like toys and pool equipment. If there are steps from the garage to the basement for the ease of transporting seasonal outdoor furniture, play them up, too.

Don't forget to declutter all closets and storage areas. Linen closets should be organized and have neatly folded sheets and towels. If the closets are overfilled, declutter! Donate items no longer needed.

Number 5: Make the Entire Home Inviting!

The fifth thing buyers want: a place that feels like home! Declutter and spruce things up. Tap into inexpensive and classic products to add visual value to the home. While upgrading a heating system or windows and doors is great, buyers can't really appreciate the money spent, unless advertised in the marketing materials.

When selling a home, the easier way to show value is simple: through quality features that everyone can appreciate. So add some wood moldings, wainscot and trim to plain staircases, hallways and walls. Play up flooring that is classic and timeless by adding some beautiful rugs. Remove trendy, very personalized or loud colors and products. Long-lasting durable flooring products such as a beautiful porcelain tile, or a classic granite or marble can create a very luxurious look. The timeless traditional styling of hardwood floors also remains very popular as it is enjoyed in the entire house. Carpeting, from a commercial low-pile to a plush high-pile design, is still in demand. Marble and limestone remain options that are favored in smaller areas. The new water-resistant wood-vinyl plank floors are gaining consumer approval, especially in the kitchen.

On the outside, decks made from wood alternative products that are eco-friendly and require less maintenance continue to grow in popularity. Eco-friendly fiber cement siding and stone veneer is replacing real wood and stone. Landscaping with less grass and more plants that require less watering remain the way of the future. Buyers also love a home equipped with smart home technology from locks, switches, speakers and more. So make sure the sales agent demonstrates these items during a showing. Remember: if you want top dollar for your home, it has to look top dollar!

7

Think Like a Department Store and Market a Lifestyle

As stated in previous chapters, HGTV changed what buyers expect when shopping for a home. Although it is unrealistic to think everyone's home has rooms that look like a department store display, that is the new reality for today's sellers. Gone are the days of having a home look somewhat cluttered, slightly unattractive, and too much a reflection of one's personality. More than ever before, people assume that they have "a right" to live well. Millennials, in particular, expect more, especially if they lived in a nicely appointed home with their parents. When they prepare to buy their first home, will it be suited for their lifestyle, including video gaming and multiple computer screens for reading a book while checking email? What about empty nester and move-up buyers who bring lots of furniture with them, such as dining and living room sets? Will furniture placement be suitable for the entertaining they may want to do?

Today's buyers are savvy home shoppers, thanks to Internet access to real estate and media attention to the home buying process. For example, townhouses are especially appealing to single people and empty nesters as well as those with a young family, as they don't require owners to repair buildings or maintain landscaping, which are typically covered by community maintenance fees.

Stylish architecture, flexible floor space and reliable, name brand home products are also important. With appliances known to not last as long as they use to, buyers like homes with easy to use whole house warranties to counterbalance the possibility of one of them breaking down. Community amenities remain appealing. Buyers continue to appreciate things that can promote their lifestyle needs and other things that they might never find by living in a stand-alone home nor within a planned community setting. For example, many enjoy tennis courts, walking and jogging paths, swimming pools, and other leisurely pursuits. Why? Because you are never just selling a home, you are selling a lifestyle!

A No-Nonsense Review of My Top Ten Home and Lifestyle Marketing Tips

• There are plenty of books written on how to declutter a home, so get organized, from outside to inside the closets, basement and garage. Don't forget the linen closets; fold the towels like seen in a store—nice and tight, no loose corners. Never overstuff linen closets with too many towels, blankets and sheets! Never overstuff a pantry with too much bulk food! Paint a cement garage floor to prevent the pumice from adhering to the bottom of shoes and damaging the floors inside a home.

• Potential buyers may open the refrigerator, microwave, dishwasher, medicine cabinet and pantry—so be prepared and get them cleaned up! Buyers can be very judgmental about a seller's cleanliness! They prefer an "easy to clean" lifestyle. This can't be seen if a home screams with dirty walls, cracked grout, switch plates covered in grime, and food particles in and on the kitchen cabinets.

• Securely store all valuables, such as jewelry, money and expensive art work. In the world of real estate, there are few reported cases of theft while showing a home, but that doesn't mean to forget about placing all valuables out of sight. There are more reported cases of people trying to steal prescription drugs, especially pain medications, so secure them.

• Virtual Staging is growing in popularity. If deciding to use it, do it only as a last resort. Why? Like me and many others, we continue to struggle with totally embracing this concept for one simple reason: potential buyers may be able to see what a house could look like with furniture in digitally enhanced images, but when they get to the house, there is no furniture. People buy based on first impressions and emotions. It is an especially emotional experience to see a nicely appointed home, and an empty house just doesn't fully help a lot of buyers fall in love with a home.

• Present a home with well-placed furniture and accessories. Even if you think the home looks beautiful to you, it may not be to the targeted buyers. If the home already has great furniture and accessories, be sure these pieces are being utilized correctly. For example, many sellers are repurposing their living room and dining room. They are taking the oversized living room and making it a dining room so they can accommodate over a dozen guests at one time for those yearly holiday parties. The dining room is often transformed into a library/sitting room for smaller parties. And remember, scale back (no need to eliminate) pictures of the loved ones.

• Think KITCHEN. I can't stress this enough. The kitchen is the most important room in the house. It's the heart of the home. Make this room look its best. The kitchen is the home's daily gathering place. There should be no compromising on its design. As an example, if the home has 30-year-old, worn out countertops, but nice classic or vintage cabinets, try to install new countertops before listing.

• Think MASTER BEDROOM. "Oh honey, I just love this master bedroom, it's romantic and relaxing." If your master bedroom doesn't portray that, get to work on making it "sex-ready." Yes, the master bedroom remains the number one place for making babies, so put away that ugly plaid bedspread and any reference to religion, kids or work.

• Have a mix of good and bad furniture? Ditch the ugly, old junk and keep the nice stuff including vintage pieces.

• Design 101: pair a vintage dresser with a contemporary lamp. As with married couples, opposites attract. When it comes to color, consider: gray/orange, brown/green, black/white, etc. Tone on tone colors (for example, off-white walls with off-white furniture and accessories) can look very dramatic. If everything in the room is of a smooth surface, add texture. If everything in a room is the same height, add something tall to break up the space. If the ceilings are only eight feet, install drapes from floor to ceiling (not just to the window height) to make the room look bigger. When displaying objects, taller ones belong in back with smaller ones in front.

• If a sales agent does not have experience in staging and the house is not the best it can be, consider hiring a stager.

 Consider displaying today's popular adult beverages appropriately positioned somewhere in the home. A bottle of champagne with a set of nice flutes displayed in a proper area can help potential buyers envision popping it open after they purchase the home. Display some beer bottles with decorative beer steins on the coffee table in the family room to help potential buyers envision a boys' or girls' night of poker, sports games or old movies.

Get Into the Home Selling and Marketing Mindset: Think Like a Builder!

What? Contemplate how great it would be to make a home look like a builder's furnished model. Builders create homes designed with lots of lifestyle amenities, because they know it sells homes faster and for more money! They use models that are fully decorated to help buyers EXPERIENCE the home's modern conveniences, spaces and features. Want to know what buyers desire and how to make a home ready to sell in today's unpredictable marketplace? Take the time to visit some model homes in the area, if available, or go online to a national builder's website to see what's being built around the country. Developers know that a fully or partially furnished model home is a necessary marketing tool. Whether targeting the lifestyle of singles, families, active adults or seniors, a beautifully decorated and merchandized home affords potential buyers the opportunity to envision themselves living in that single-family home, townhouse or condominium in the countryside, suburbs or city, or by a golf course, near an ocean or lake.

The Top Ten Things Successful Builders Do When Marketing a New Home Community

•   An experienced developer knows that it takes a team of professionals to create that model home, including an architect, project manager, sales and marketing staff and interior merchandiser/designer. It also requires research from former purchasers and consumers to formulate ideas for a community which can often be obtained via focus groups or questionnaires. Recognizing the importance of price, size, value and quality as well as architectural appointments helps the team better compile the necessary and special features needed to create the ideal "lifestyle" home for their targeted market.

•   Because buyers have become very savvy home shoppers, what were once considered "options" have now become standard features in many homes. Homes have tall ceilings, ample windows, fireplaces and architectural details as well as sumptuous master bathrooms, dramatic entry foyers, bright functional kitchens, exciting gathering rooms and extra high ceilings in the basements. And depending on the buyer's lifestyle and budget, today's furnished model home will often showcase a finished basement with a well-appointed media room, home office, game room, play area or second kitchen for grandparents or returning children.

•   Builders know new homes need to be designed not only with superior craftsmanship, high quality structural materials and energy-efficient products, but also with exterior curb appeal, state-of-the-art interior features and ample lifestyle space in order to appeal to the variety of buyers shopping for a new home. Sometimes it's not always easy to incorporate the latest technology. For example, solar panels can be a great way to save on energy costs, but builders are not always amenable to using them because solar panels can be costly to install, they require correct sunlight sources and they are not always accurately reflected in an appraisal of a home.

•   The all-important master bedroom and bathroom need separate space for sleeping and separate space for things like exercise equipment. For older adults, builders provide the master bath with a one-piece fiberglass shower with a built-in seat and grab bar. All buyers require bedrooms and bathrooms designed with ample storage space and room for furniture placement. They know to design a bedroom so that the bed can be positioned on the wall most easily seen when entering the room. It may or may not appeal to the Feng Shui buyer, but most buyers prefer a great, inviting bed directly across from the entry door.

•   For today's builders, they know that once they have established the home's design elements, the design team then needs to properly decide on which new products and colors to select. Since the building industry is continually introducing new advances, and there are so many different types of buyers, the decisions must be as accurate as possible. For utilitarian reasons, it's not surprising that most consumers prefer monochromatic colors in both the kitchen and bathroom for permanently installed products, like tubs, sinks and toilets.

•   For the latest products, builders know that granite and marble countertops are still the rage for the kitchen and owner's bathroom as well as non-porous quartz products. Properly sealed wood and copper countertops along with concrete and stainless steel countertops are also gaining in popularity. Stainless steel and shades of grey still lead the trend in appliance colors, followed by black. Homebuyers still have a love affair with hardwood floors on the first floor, due to traffic, and in the bedrooms because some buyers suffer from allergies. Most buyers believe wood flooring to be a good long-term investment. The most popular flooring in the foyer continues to be some form of tile, followed by hardwood. Older buyers are most concerned with practical, durable, low-maintenance flooring. Wood vinyl plank floors that look like wood and are textured and water resistant continue to grow in popularity as the technology keeps improving its durability and aesthetic appearance.

•   Buyers especially prefer maple and cherry wooden cabinets, and, to a lesser extent, oak and non-wood material in colors ranging from natural to spice. Carpet runners on wood steps with wrought iron rails are in vogue. For any buyer, hardwood floors or vinyl wood plank floors in the kitchen and powder room remain strong in appeal. Trends are also being seen with reclaimed wood. Homes are being designed with a feature wall of reclaimed wood. Reclaimed sliding barn doors can be found hanging as a walk-in closet door of the master retreat and as the pantry door in the kitchen.

•   The building industry has learned from recent research that people now place lifestyle near the top of their "wish list." So today's builders are offering value and design as well as incentives to purchase many of their "wish list" items now, verses later. This good marketing technique helps sell houses, since builders know that buyers need to "feel" an emotional attachment to the homes of their dreams, and this cannot be achieved by viewing flat, two-dimensional architectural blueprints or furnishing the home with the least expensive items.

•   Builders also understand that older and young buyers with children are very practical people. They like powder rooms designed with vanities, not pedestals, because they provide more storage. Lever faucets are more popular than knobs. Pewter and chrome plumbing fixtures are more practical and popular than brass. Porcelain sinks are more popular with older buyers than stainless steel sinks because they like the brighter colors and the ease of removing water stains. Tiles that look like wood are more practical in a kitchen than real wood floors. Glass tiles are also trendy, but need to be used in good taste and with a timeless design.

•   Since builders know that most buyers like to "feel" the space, here are a few more examples of how builders create the "look" for their targeted buyers. Active adults want to see models that reflect what they can do in their home, particularly those not working as much or spending more time on hobbies and leisurely pursuits. Models are decorated using very specific themes. For example, to appeal to a single woman, perhaps widowed, a smaller model can be decorated in a garden theme using colorful floral window coverings in the kitchen and showing lots of fresh flowers throughout the home. To help the retired businessman or busy attorney find comfort in his new home, a model can show a home office or study designed with deep grey walls, accented by a beautiful Oriental rug, displayed with a chess board. To capture the sailing spirit of potential buyers, builders will often decorate a model in shades of ocean blue, sunny yellow, sandy beige and white shells with lots of ships and boats. Many adults, especially aging baby boomers, are on a quest to find the perfect travel destination. To cater to this important pursuit, builders will decorate a model in a traveler theme, complete with maps and mugs and lots of memories.

Sales associates who have worked in the new home construction industry are generally trained in customer service, wholesale supplier and contractor sources, staging (what we used to call merchandizing a home), marketing brochures, engineering and architectural plans, just to name a few. I also remember the days of needing to clean mud from a new home before an open house, something everyone in new construction gets used to doing. Much to my surprise, many agents in the resale business would never think to help a seller get his house ready for his open house if the need arises. Think again!

Display high-end department stores' boxes and bags in the closets. It's a great way for potential buyers to connect emotionally to the home.

When a home is being shown, play some music and make sure that the house not only looks good, but smells good, too. If you smoke in the house, consider using an ionizer. Buyers get very turned off by smoke smells, especially those buyers with young children.

People bring lots of memories from their previous homes. They don't always know that great new memories will be made in their new homes. Invite them to sit around, for example, by the fireplace, to enjoy the ease and beauty of gas log flames and warmth (rather than the smell and mess associated with wood logs).

8

The Ugly Side of Home Selling

What's wrong with my home? The answer may be: plenty! Can anything be done? Absolutely!

For home owners struggling with a problematic home, it's very important to have a serious conversation about the relationship that may or may not be enjoyed with the home. Convey any and all loves and hates of home ownership to the sales agent. By articulating any fears, unresolved issues or anxieties held by anyone living in the household, a good agent can better determine the root cause of why the home may be difficult to sell. There are two common reasons for having a very unpopular home. The first is if the owners are financially and/or emotionally challenged. Generally speaking, they either don't have the willpower to clean things up or they don't have the money to fix things up. The second problem with an unpopular home occurs when owners keep delaying the listing of the home or keep finding ways to disagree about how to list it. Two common roadblocks: not being able to move anything, from a chair to a painting, in order to photograph a room, and not being allowed to place a "for sale" sign on the property. When this happens, remind the sellers of this mantra: if you don't help me; I can't help you. If after many compassionate talks to raise everyone's self-confidence and dozens of big hugs for support, it's still not possible to secure a greater working relationship between sales agent and sellers—walk away! Find another agent or seller—don't settle! Don't give up hope— be strong! Let's get started with the many homes that might be the most difficult to sell and how they can get sold.

The Ugly House

If it's truly an ugly, outdated or unusual home located in a nice town with good schools, it's entirely possible an investor, whether an experienced builder/remodeler or inexperienced flipper, may be willing to buy the home. Of course, the price will be at a deep discount because homes become devalued when sellers can no longer keep it in good condition. That said, don't feel like these are the only sellers with issues; plenty of sellers have similar stories. Remember: it feels good to bring professionalism and empathy to families in need of selling an undesirable home. Many in real estate have seen, heard about or experienced far more than we choose to admit. As an example, I had one middle-aged female seller greet me at the door in her underwear (she was off her medications at the time). I politely requested that she never do that again. I also had a client who accidentally left his dog in the basement, and it died! He then asked me to remove it; I said no! I had yet another client who asked me to sell her parents' home knowing the house wasn't hers to sell; I walked away!

Write in the listing, "The sellers are very motivated." The house may be ugly, but by indicating they are interested in any offers, potential buyers won't be afraid of the challenge to buy.

My Home Is in the Wrong Location

So the home sits on a busy street, or worse yet, a major highway, or even worse than that, in a flood zone, a sinkhole area or a dangerous neighborhood. Unless the real estate market remains very good in the area, the home can be destined to take longer to sell, if it can sell at all. A home in a bad location, but with a beautiful interior and correctly priced, has a better chance of selling than a house in a bad location, in ugly condition and priced too high.

If a home is subject to highway noise, turn that negative into a positive. Here are a few examples: indicate how it is a short drive to work, very private or quiet when inside. Quiet the outside noises that might infiltrate the home's interior. Purchase insulated drapes for the windows, decorate the walls with padded fabric or have a music system that can be heard throughout the house.

If a home is in a flood plain, take the best preventative measures, such as installing a sophisticated drainage system and a whole house generation, to avert a flood condition to the home and include the literature about the system in the listing.

Someone Passed Away in the Home; It's Haunted!

Lots of sad as well as happy things happen in homes across the country every day. If a home experienced a very sad event, such as suicide or murder, should it be disclosed? Some state laws say it does not have to be disclosed, some states do require disclosure. Here's my take, for those states, like New Jersey, that do not have to disclose. Would it be okay if the buyers found out from the next door neighbor after they moved in? Suppose the buyers' belief system does not allow them to live in a home where a death occurred? Do you really want to go through the financial and emotional trauma of being sued if the buyers decide to do so? The death of a person living in a home remains a tough sell for most, so consider how that negative can be turned into a positive. For example, taking care of an elderly person who dies naturally in the home can be seen as caring sellers who have empathy for the sick or elderly.

 Some buyers love living near a cemetery because they like the idea of being near a park-like setting with quiet (albeit departed) neighbors. If a home sits near an historical cemetery, artists and historians often see great value in living in this setting.

The Old People's Home

It proves difficult to sell a dated, senior citizen home in "as is" condition, especially in a buyers' market, so try to update within reason. I prefer not to determine a "fix-up" budget based on a percentage of the home's value, since each home requires a different figure. My advice: make the budget as low as possible while making the home as nice as possible.

Many homes of older people are inherited by a relative or friend. Some of these homes are located in communities created especially for the 55 and older crowd, as well as those living in vacation destinations. Often, these homes are listed considerably under their value because the children inherit their parents' home and don't have the knowledge or desire to sell up! An entire chapter on shared personal experiences with the estates of older or deceased parents can be found next.

 Seniors may have accumulated lots of possessions during their lifetime, and they often have very nice antique furniture, collectibles and art work in their

home. Use these pieces in conjunction with contemporary lamps and art; it's a great way to appeal to today's
younger buyers.

The Reverse Mortgage Home

Reverse mortgages continue to grow in popularity for those wanting more money while on a fixed income and desirous of aging in their own home. The homes are
usually sold by the surviving children of the parents with the idea that they will receive
some equity from the sale of the property. Unfortunately, some heirs aren't aware or
don't provide disclosure of what the home can be sold for without it becoming a short
sale (i.e., the seller owes more than the house is worth). As a seller, disclose to the sales
agent what amount of money needs to be realized after the sale, including real estate
commissions, taxes, liens, etc. that need to be paid. If a sales agent, don't take the listing until reliable documentation from the lending institution is produced and there
has been a conversation with the bank to confirm the house can be sold, including any
time constraints for the sale.

It feels good to bring professionalism and
empathy to family members in need of selling their home with a reverse mortgage. By
patiently working with loved ones who may
have just lost a father or mother, it's possible
to sell up!

The Distressed Home

Pre-foreclosure (short sales) and foreclosure homes, including a sheriff sale,
handing back the deed and walking away (deed in lieu) and real estate owned (REO)
bank properties continue to bombard some communities across America. Vacant
and abandoned homes as well as occupied homes in disrepair gather like war planes
on a runway, antagonizing recovering housing markets by keeping home prices in a
holding pattern. How can real estate professionals and homeowners survive and rally
their neighborhood market back to victory? The crisis families feel as a result of being
forced to sell their homes can be very intense. The two big reasons: homeowners feel
embarrassed and ashamed, and agents feel frustrated and overworked.

So let's review the challenges; it's all in the details! Sales agents can face a myriad of problems when selling short sales, including the possibility of bank-induced
decreased commissions. A short sale occurs when the seller can no longer afford to
pay the mortgage and owes more than it is worth at the time of sale. The seller must
complete many documents and make numerous phone calls, along with their sales
agent, in order to seek approval for an offer of sale. The marketing documents must
be very informational; good pictures remain essential and the correct price for the
home must be carefully considered. Everyone seems to have heard countless horror
stories about the length of time lenders take to approve a pre-foreclosure property.
Don't let that stop an agent who understands what it takes to list a short sale. Yes, it
can take an extended amount of time, especially lots of phone calls with the lender.

Remember: many people are involved in order to process a lender's pre-foreclosure paperwork; never assume one department knows what the other department is doing. It also helps to ensure that the sellers have a good attorney with short sale experience. It proves very time consuming to market distressed properties. It really helps if there is someone to make all the calls, process all the paperwork and exhibit the persistence needed to get short sales closed. Encourage other agents to sell short sales and become SFR certified through their local real estate board. The sooner these homes get off the market, the quicker distressed markets can recover. Sellers and agents should stay proactive throughout the process. Ask lenders to work with you (not against you) to make the short sale process less painful. Sales agents should always encourage families to seek help from counseling centers, friends or houses of worship in order to overcome the emotional strain of losing their homes. Sales agents, it can truly feel good knowing how to help homeowners before losing their homes to foreclosure. When help exists, hope can heal. We as a real estate community can and must come together to preserve dignity and respect sellers need, while they work through a highly emotional crisis when forced to sell their home. To learn more, go to www.making-homeaffordable.gov.

Sales associates need to be patient, honest and consolatory. They also need to avert their own "burn-out" caused by the emotional strain of working with homeowners who are vulnerable to adversity.

Losing Your Home—the Reality of It

After losing a home, it often proves very difficult to transition from owner to renter. After years of investing in a home, from purchasing nice furniture and living a comfortable lifestyle to making neighborhood friends, it's very painful to have it all taken away. But perhaps even more difficult is the psychological affect this crisis creates on an entire family, especially on children. Ever present: stress, depression, anger, yelling and lots of sleepless nights worrying about the future. As with a death in the family or divorce, when faced with the devastation of losing a home, it is much easier to procrastinate about everything. It really helps to find support from people who can help move things forward. It remains especially difficult if children are involved. Talk with them frequently and seek professional counseling when necessary. Parents or spouses feel a tremendous sense of defeat and a diminished sense of self-worth. Sales agents need to talk about the crisis and help where possible. Try to understand how the sellers think. They may be very fearful and scared. Most importantly, every person copes with adversity in a different way, and each distressed seller provides a unique perspective. Most distressed home sellers do not have the financial resources to make any repairs to their home, forcing them to sell their home "as is." In addition, they are losing their biggest investment along with any equity obtained during ownership, so the reality of having to lose so much takes a tremendous toll. My advice is simple: minimize as much of the trauma as possible. Unfortunately, some distressed homeowners simply can't cope at all. They can't talk about it, and they can't act upon it. Rather than sell, they procrastinated until that dreaded day comes.....the sheriff sale notice. Don't become emotionally crippled; don't panic and walk away! Remember, a sheriff sale will not go away once the complaint gets served. The foreclosure process begins unless the homeowners act to resolve it. Try and get it resolved!

A distressed home sale produces a huge amount of stress; it can cause break-ups, divorce, childhood illnesses, depression and even death. The devastation of losing a home can be less damaging if homeowners with diminished income create an early selling strategy, and if not emotionally possible, then seek a dignified solution while moving through the foreclosure process.

9

When It's Time to Sell Your Parents' Home

Like most sellers or sales agents, I thought myself to be a fairly astute sales and marketing professional for just about any type of home. Unfortunately, my nearly 40 years of experience at the time could not help me cope with the grueling, often combative discussions with my family on how to market my parents' home of 40 years, and the physically-exhausting, 12-hour days (often without help) while trying to organize the home and clear it out. I turned into a crazy person during the process, but the adversity made me even stronger and more determined to successfully sell my parents' home.

My personal account of selling my parents' home is not unique, but it's my true story, and, hopefully, it can provide solace and strength if faced with the same challenge. And for those who will manage a peaceful settlement of their parents' estate, I commend you!

Step 1: Clean, Organize and Update

It took three months to clean, organize and update my parents' very charming, 1946, Cape Cod architectural style home. It was filled with many possessions and took nearly two weeks just to de-clutter. Seniors save a lot of stuff! All dated, ugly furniture went to charity, and all family photographs went back to family and friends. Since seniors tend to love loud, bright colors, the entire home got a fresh coat of neutral paint colors from grey to beige and white. All outdated and ugly light fixtures got replaced with attractive, name-brand models. Vintage door knobs and cabinet hardware got restored. Smells of mothballs and other foul odors that originally filled the home were eliminated. Grease and crud that covered the kitchen and bathrooms received a thorough cleaning, including the grout, and were updated with new plumbing fixtures and countertops. With old, dirty carpets removed, the wood floors got a much needed polish. Laughingly, I learned how to remove crud with my fingernails and that crud comes in many forms: grease crud from cooking, dirt crud from not cleaning, and basement crud that comes from who knows where. Thank goodness it's possible to buy a cleaning product specifically designed to remove crud! I recommend Krud Kutter — it really works!

Step II: Staging

Since it's very difficult to sell a dated, senior citizen home in "as is" condition in a buyers' market or possibly any market (except at a deep discount), I tried to return my parents' home back to new, but within a reasonable budget of $5000. Note that every budget is different, because it is based on labor costs, materials needed and the extent of the updating. After visits from the plumber, painter and handy husbands and extended family, the much needed updates to the home were completed. The home was decorated for our targeted buyers: first-timers. All kinds of hip and youthful accessories were chosen so new owners could picture themselves enjoying a cute, charming kitchen and a sexy bedroom and bathroom. Accessories were one step above their income level. Some of the better sofas and chairs were used to decorate the family room. With the home looking move-in ready and the marketing materials (described in more detail in Chapter 10) beautifully created, the home sold within five days at close to asking price!

Step III: Lessons Learned

So what can be learned from this experience?

If you have a sibling or siblings to deal with, understand that some siblings may not have the resources or time. Accept this, and do what needs to be done to get the home ready for sale.

Never complain about the amount of hours put into cleaning/repairing/organizing. Remember, it doesn't matter. This work is being done because of the love felt towards your parents.

If possible, put in writing what each family member agrees to do and have everyone agree on a time line. If someone doesn't do their job, agree that it will be performed by hired help and paid for by the person who was too busy working or lived too far away to perform the work.

Seniors in failing health live differently; don't judge them. You must make the home look good in order sell it fast, and sell it at the best possible price.

Everyone grieves differently, especially after the death of a parent. Estate sales can be overly emotional for some siblings, especially when it comes to personal items that evoke memories of their usage. Even a dirty, torn chair from a mother's desk can be difficult to part with.

Be very careful when dividing up personal items between family members. Find reputable antique and collectible dealers through referrals.

And finally, don't hold a grudge against family members. Love them for who they are even if it's difficult to agree on how to sell your parents' home.

If there are handicapped-related items in the home, such as a shower grip or built-in shower chair, some buyers may find that appealing, so indicate them in the marketing materials.

10

The New Age of Marketing

Once upon a time in the world of real estate, sales agents looked at paper copies of home listings found in big printed binders and books. Agents would never miss an opportunity to put clients in their cars to preview homes. Buyers were pre-qualified for a mortgage by agents. Mortgage representatives were at the bank expecting a visit from buyers needing to be pre-approved for a loan. Home shoppers poured over the newspaper every Sunday to circle or highlight each home to be seen that day. Open houses proved entertaining for many home seekers. Oh yes, there were lots of folks found pretending to be looking for a five-bedroom mansion when all they could afford was a one-bedroom condo! Broker open houses on any given weekday provided agents with a supportive and fun social event often around trays of delicious foods.

There was a cornucopia of new homes and furnished model homes to see. Everyone from potential buyers to curiosity seekers craved the latest in architectural styles and interior design trends. For those builders who could afford it, billboards and radio advertising hoped to excite potential buyers to come out in droves on any given Sunday afternoon for a look at the latest in new home construction in some of the prettiest places on earth.

So what's changed? The Internet! Paperless communication and advertising became the new way of shopping for homes. That said, it's still possible to find newspapers and magazines that advertise homes for sale and Sunday television shows advertising (mostly high-end) real estate sales. People still attend open houses, but before they do, the vast majority start their home search on the Internet.

It can be challenging to navigate the ever-changing Internet. Don't be intimidated; here's a concise overview of my top ten marketing tips that prove critical to getting a home sold faster and for more money.

Google It!

Google Maps allow potential buyers to zoom in on any home that catches their fancy. If a home was built in a bad location, chances are potential buyers will know before they go. On the flip side, buyers won't need to waste sellers' time, if they don't like the land, street or community.

Sellers and agents should also Google the address of the home being listed to see how many sites may have incorrect information. Note: over the years, criticism circulated around sites like Zillow and Trulia due to inaccuracy of information. A Zillow Zestimate is just that, an estimate and Zillow does include a disclaimer that prices may not be accurate. On the flip side, Zillow provides interesting marketplace facts. For example, did you know the first two weeks in May are when, according to Zillow, the greatest number of buyers make their offers?

Keep a home sale "genuine." If there is something bad about the home, like living near a busy school playground, figure out a way to demonstrate the positive side of that issue.

You Can't Sell a Home if the Buyers Can't Buy It—the Pre-Approval Letter

Remember, the goal is to get a home seen by more qualified buyers! Savvy sales agents know to never take out clients to see homes for sale unless they possess a pre-approval letter from a reputable lender. This ensures they can afford the home of their dreams and qualify to repay the mortgage. Don't waste time and energy; don't bring clients who are not qualified. Lenders have made it easier than ever to determine if buyers qualify for a loan due to their online qualifying procedures. Want to review a generic mortgage app; there are a plethora of mortgage calculation apps available online. And finally, not all lenders are created equal; shop around for a lender who knows the market. It is not uncommon to have a sale fall apart because the lender could not get the home closed on time.

A good lender will provide a home listing with mortgage information for potential buyers, include it as part of the marketing materials. By having a flyer with examples of different down payment options, potential buyers can see what it would cost to live in the home each month. Consider a sheet titled "Renting vs. Buying" and show the different options.

Buyers Start Their Home Search With Primary Online Home Listing Sites

Where buyers choose to begin their online home search depends on their particular like or dislike for any given real estate site. Obviously, the easier it is to navigate the site, the more people will use it. Popular real estate databases include local, regional and state multiple listing site; national real estate sites like Zillow and Trulia (the top two in the country) as well as Yahoo!Homes and REALTOR.com; plus national brokerage websites, such as ColdwellBanker.com. A sales agent should be using as many online available resources as possible. And don't forget to consider smaller, specialized database sites, such as OldHouses.com, which list historical homes.

Never miss an opportunity to provide the maximum number of images allowable and/or video of the home, because it matters. The more photographs, plus the inclusion of a video, the higher the position among similar listings can be achieved on listing sites, such as Zillow and Trulia. Be at the top of a potential buyer's search results!

Local multiple listing sites often allow descriptions for each picture of the home. It's not always easy to understand a picture without a caption, so ensure each picture comes with the most important details of what is being shown. For example, wood floors, porcelain tile, etc.

Social Media: The Secondary Home Listing Sites

Facebook, Instagram and Twitter have created platforms for real estate agents to promote homes for sale. My favorite: Facebook. Facebook makes it so easy for agents to "boost" a home listing. It's relatively inexpensive compared to print advertising. Plus, with Facebook it's possible to run an ad campaign directed at specific towns, age groups and interests of the targeted buyers. Agents can also create a Facebook page for a listing. How effective is the process? I targeted potential buyers within a certain age group for one of my listings, and they came to my open house.

There are plenty of other options to consider on the Internet. Agents can create a blog for a home or put a listing on their blog or business page. Business people use LinkedIn and often agents will advertise a listing on this site. Just make sure to select the most appropriate sites, because it's possible to run ads just about everywhere on the Internet.

 Not comfortable navigating the Internet? Consider hiring a professional consultant with Internet experience to market the home.

Meaningful Email and Paper Mailings

Not everyone is online. Not everyone likes Twitter, Facebook, LinkedIn and other social media platforms. Sending out a paper mailing, through the use of a flyer, can sometimes lead to a buyer, especially older buyers who like receiving mail. Remember: take good pictures of the home to create an emotional response from the viewers and add eye-catching wording, like call-to-action phases, such as "call me for a showing." Of course, real estate, home and lifestyle magazines, as well as newspapers (print and online) need to be considered as possible marketing venues if that is where the targeted buyers like to shop for homes.

Emails can also be the perfect vehicle for advertising a home to those who choose to enjoy information coming through their "in-box." There are so many ways to send a home listing via email. I find it easier and less expensive to send bulk emails to other agents and to potential buyers. It's very simple to hire a company to send email advertising to targeted agents. Listing alerts by companies, such as Property Blasts Homes and Send My Listing, can design a professional looking email that includes details of the home. The general problem with most of these email service companies is that they send the viewer to a link to view the images of the home. Pictures and video files are generally too large in size for email usage, which is why it's difficult to include pictures of the home. Unfortunately, it proves difficult to capture viewers with just words and no pictures of the home. Remember why: because it's the house that sells the house. If there are no pictures of the house in the email, it reduces the viewers' chance of completely understanding the house and wanting to open the email for more details.

 If advertising a home via email, make sure the subject line says something very appealing to the targeted buyers. Think like an advertising agency and create a catchy headline. My favorite tag words usually incorporate the words "come home" and sometimes I create fun tag lines like, "Your dog will thank you for buying this home."

TYPOS Are a No-No When Promoting a Home

We all make typos from time-to-time. It's possible to find some in my book! Whether in print or online marketing, ensure the home facts get typed correctly. Double check every site that is advertising the listing. And one more thing: do use the correct terms for products in the home. For example, when describing a jetted tub, do not use Jacuzzi ® or Whirlpool; they are name brands. Do not confuse a jetted tub in the bathroom with a hot tub, a free-standing, jetted water enclosure generally designed for an outside application.

As stated earlier, create a vivid description of the home so that it appeals to the targeted buyers. Use this description for local multiple listing sites as well as national sites used to advertise the home for sale. Try to be as specific as possible. For example, if it's known the targeted buyers will appreciate smart home technology, advertise it. Don't be afraid to be creative; but don't be in violation of state real estate laws. Lastly, remember to list anything not included with the home, such as an heirloom chandelier. Never assume buyers know it will not stay with the house.

 Buyers love "widespread storage" and "move-in ready", so use these key descriptive words in the advertising campaign, if applicable.

Sincere Pictures With a Story

STOP, I repeat STOP, photographing rooms with wide angle lenses! No one wants to come to a house and discover the rooms are smaller than the images. It's a real turnoff. If a room is small, simply remove some furniture and make sure the walls are painted a light neutral color. If it proves difficult to photograph small spaces, here are some suggestions: photograph each room from several different vantage points. Photograph "vignettes" (small designed areas) of each room which highlight the best and most exciting features of the room. Some agents use virtual staging photographs for a vacant home. It can be helpful, especially when showing the before and after images and incorporating all of the photographs into the marketing materials. I'm not a big fan, because virtual staging photography can be a disappointment when potential buyers arrive to an empty house. As stated before, it's the house that sells the house.

Besides photographing the interior, don't forget to take outdoor images of the landscaping and the front entrance. If there are interesting walkways, a nice pool or any outdoor or community amenities, take pictures of them too. If it's not possible to find enough images to meet the maximum required for all the sites the home will be featured on, take detailed images of pretty things. For example, photograph nice looking faucets and shower heads. Take pictures of utilitarian features, like the furnace and air conditioning units, especially if in good condition.

Not everyone is using or can afford to consider aerial photograph with the use of a drone, or 3-D Matterport camera images, or evening pics with landscape lighting. If possible, add them to the marketing campaign.

Vivid Videos Devoid of Distractions

When creating a video of a home consider showing those features that can't really be expressed in photographs. A video, as with photographs, is part of the pre-selling, marketing process. The idea is to get potential buyers excited about the house and get them so emotionally connected that they want to see it in person. Music with a video tour of the home is a great way to elevate feelings. I know lots of sales agents think walking through the home in their video is a great way to show it. I don't agree with that idea; it's a distraction. It is better to add music and a voice over to explain the home's appeal to the targeted buyers. That said; it is a great idea to include a person or people when conveying a lifestyle. For example, create a video around cooking in the kitchen with friends, especially if potential buyers may find it difficult to envision the scope and size of the entertaining space. Host the party using Facebook Live. My favorite—create a drone video of the exterior of the home and community. It's a dramatic way to showcase a home with an interesting roof top, streetscapes and topography.

Filming a home allows potential buyers the opportunity to feel the spaces and get emotionally involved with the tour. Unless there is no budget or you're not great at videoing with a cell phone; hire a professional for the video shoot. Video can then be shared on social media and real estate sites. My favorite place to post home videos: Facebook. You see it and then click on it to play. My favorite second place to post is YouTube. It is a public site and, like Facebook, it indicates how many sets of eyes viewed it. Can't afford a professional video? There are dozens of free apps to consider for creating and editing a photo slideshow to music or a video to music. My favorite is Quik. There are more private ways to send a video too, like Dropbox. Some high end listings prefer to do a video and copy it onto a DVD or flash drive which can be mailed anywhere.

Make the Marketing Materials Memorable

As stated earlier, think like a builder and create an exciting brochure for the home. It doesn't have to be expensive, especially if on a limited budget. It can be a four-color brochure printed on copy paper, and don't forget to create an electronic version of it and any accompanying flyers. What should be included in the brochure: Pictures, Multiple Listing Sheet, Features List (list all the products and dates of installation, if known), Amenities List (walk paths, playground, etc.) and Added Value Features (trendy add-ons to the home that appeal to the targeted buyers). Add a flyer about the town to include schools, houses of worship and fun facts, like famous people who use to live in the town. Good schools attract people with kids. Reprint reports on the schools' good records. Get letters of testament from neighbors. Add a mortgage calculator flyer. If the community has a newsletter, include in the marketing materials.

Add a seller's disclosure, if available. Abide by the real estate commission for advertising whether print media, social media or videos. And lastly, be careful; include a disclaimer to any marketing materials used to sell a home. Consider adding, "subject to errors and omissions."

Helpful Human Feedback

Face-to-face contact with a house, the listing agent, the buyers and the sellers remain most important no matter how much money is spent on Internet presence, print materials or email advertising. When accessing a home's competition, agents need to see every listing in person, especially the direct competition, to better access all conditions not seen online. The same is true for buyers, who should never buy a home unless they see it. Open houses for agents and buyers can often make the difference when trying to show a house. Advice about the price of a home and the condition of a home are "gifts" received from real estate agents, buyers and other sellers. By following-up with agents who have shown the house, it's possible to get constructive feedback. Potential buyers seem to like talking to other agents about what they don't like about a house. This information needs to be conveyed to the seller.

When hosting an open house, have potential buyers sign in with Open Home Pro. It's a free app and a great way to track open house attendance.

While at the open house, one way to stay connected with guests instantly and long after they have left the house is through Facebook, Instagram and Twitter, especially with younger buyers.

11

The Creation of the Innocent Buyer

Calling Attention to the Benefits of Learning Home Safety Skills

The majority of young people prefer to find a perfect home that is move-in ready. Why is this? It's because we baby boomers contributed to this next generation of buyers' ability to purchase a home. More specifically, there has been a significant decrease in practical home and life skills in our society over the past few decades. This has created a national crisis for today's youth, and these youth are now today's buyers! So, don't skip reading this chapter; it is important information!

Do most young people really understand the benefits of learning home safety skills? If you have ever heard any of the following scenarios, then the answer is probably no. "Why should I care about mending the fence that I broke?" "Mom, the toilet is overflowing with disgusting stuff; I don't know what to do!" "Dad, my bedroom door won't stay closed; can you fix it?"

It is a national crisis when most young people don't know what to do to keep themselves and their home safe from fires, electrical problems and plumbing disasters. Parents are supposed to teach their children basic home safety, but if parents lack the skills, how will children know what to do in an emergency? Everyday practical knowledge for the home comes with education, practice and experience. Unfortunately, progress and changes in our society have contributed to the demise of the time and knowledge needed to teach our children the benefits of being their own handyman or handywoman.

With each new generation there is less time to pass on traditions, and there are fewer opportunities to teach home repair. Sadly, there is not as much family involvement with parents and grandparents these days, who understood the importance of being self-sufficient home dwellers. It is a socio-economic crisis that plagues each new generation. It has been written about over decades by scholars and educators alike, and it is played out among families in their homes or apartments each and every day.

Even if we can identify the life skills children are losing, do most kids and parents think it really matters? We don't exactly know. There is no national survey for this question, but there should be. However, one truth is known; it's hard to care or think it matters if parents don't see the benefit of knowing how to use a hammer or wrench.

Our children live in a more complicated, multi-media environment than of past generations, when it was the television and radio that occupied free time. Young adults, in particular, can be consumed by music on their listening device, talking with friends on a cell phone, connecting their computers to chat rooms or playing a video game on a big-screen TV. As a result, they can become more accustomed to less human contact and hands-on experiences around the house.

As parents, it is up to us to provide a balance in their lives between their new toys and toys that can be made with a hammer, chisel and saw. Nowadays, finding time to teach our children can be difficult and studies suggest that parents spend less time with their children by nearly 10 to 15 hours than in the 1960s. If parents don't have the time to help our youth, how will they learn to become self-sufficient adults?

Eventually, every child will leave a family home for their dorm, apartment or their own home. Will they be ready for the safety challenges that await them? Did you remember to teach them to set a timer for the lights to help prevent a burglary? Can they prevent the basement from flooding because they can recognize when to replace the old water heater? Even more importantly, can they prevent fires from happening? Will they change the furnace filter at least twice each year, remove the lint from the dryer filter after each load of laundry, and maintain a clean fireplace? If they don't, would you want to live next door to them? According to statistics, fires kill more Americans each year than natural disasters, with cooking fires being the leading cause. Not providing our children with the necessary skills to keep their homes safe puts them at risk and can also harm others.

By keeping children busy around the home with chores and providing them with training sessions in fire safety, cooking classes, gardening and sewing projects, among others, also helps to keep them more physically active. We have all heard that childhood obesity and diabetes are at an all-time high. Organizations like the YMCA, Boy and Girl Scouts, among others, encourage children to get more exercise and to learn life skills, but much more needs to be done on a national level in order to call attention to the plight of so many children who don't know why it is important to have a well-rounded education that incorporates practical, physical and intellectual learning.

Wealthy celebrities, such as Oprah Winfrey and Bill Gates, are trying to improve child education. Unfortunately, the "No Child Left Behind Act" from 2002-2015 focused on grades and scores to ensure that every child was getting a good, basic education. Many hands-on programs were eliminated. So don't assume schools are taking the time to educate their students about tools, fire safety and home ownership. Schools typically do not take on these parental roles, and should we really want them to?

Parents who are associated with construction can lead by example, but for those who are unable, they can only hope that sometime down the road, their children will learn some form of home life skills, perhaps from friends, relatives, books, apps or teachers; hopefully, before they become homeowners, and not after a basement flood or fire in the chimney! There are plenty of home shows on cable television for adults to watch that can guide them through many home safety and repair issues, but the same cannot be said for children of all ages, who do not have a home safety show to enjoy on a Saturday morning!

So what can be done? As parents, we can't force our children to enjoy playing with tools, whether real or as toys. We can't force them to remember every fire safety rule or every home maintenance tip, and we certainly can't convince them to make or fix things with their own hands. The National Kids Construction Club suggests that if your child is young, encourage hands-on fun with shovels, blocks and building toys. Go outside and explore the world by visiting a construction site, or stop and watch a sidewalk or road being constructed. Join school clubs that encourage creativity with hands-on learning. Consider a membership with youth organizations like the Boy or Girl Scouts. Encourage teens to participate in Habitat for Humanity projects, which will help them gain practical skills in home construction and technology. If their school offers practical arts courses, encourage them to enroll. Plan a visit to a hardware store with your children. Read how-to books and tackle a home repair project with your son or daughter, such as installing new tile on the laundry room floor. If you're lucky enough to have a grandparent, ask them to share their stories of the old times. Then explore your heritage by finding old pieces of furniture made by hand.

Recognizing that it is our responsibility to instill good values in our children is the first step in solving this national problem. How we teach youth about the importance of achieving a well-rounded education that includes sports, the arts, academics, technology and practical home safety training needs to begin very early. If we as parents offer help and advice, perhaps our children will listen. Studies have shown that students want to change things for the better. Why not encourage them! Visit the National Kids Construction Club's Facebook page to learn more on this subject.

12

Raising Awareness to Ethics and Code of Conduct

I'll never forget my first listing involving my sweet, elderly, frail, 85-year-old neighbor and his wife. Clients who are senior citizens in declining physical and mental health require much time and patience. They usually need a lot more time with de-cluttering their home, since they have a lifetime of memories to pack. It takes tremendous perseverance, but they usually appreciate a full-service approach to selling their home.

The personal struggles of clients with compromised mental capacities, in my professional opinion, are the most challenging type of client (whether a buyer or seller). The reason is simple; you do not know and cannot predict their psychological state of mind. It takes a lot of patience, but it helps if the client is forthcoming about their issues, such as Obsessive Compulsive Disorder and Hoarding.

I once had a client who preferred endless, agonizing visits and phone calls; this can happen when a client who was once a thriving and brilliant real estate attorney now suffers from a personality disorder. She so cleverly cloaked her seller's tactics; she convinced me to help her fix up her home and then decided not to sell.

A sweet, middle-aged client made me so sad because she suffered from pain medication addiction and needed to sell her home in order to survive (a for-sale-by-owner sale in this instance). Care should be taken to help such clients feel worthy by helping them organize their possessions and properly prepare themselves, especially while showing their home. My client once mistakenly answered the door half-dressed and in a daze. Just remember to treat such clients with dignity and respect.

The selling of a parent's home during an estate sale, especially in a challenging housing market, can also present difficult compromises. Surviving children experience grief for a great deal of time, and disagreeing on a list or sale price between the siblings can lead to a dispute. Often, no outlet exists for their grief but to vent through you, the listing agent, in order to release their pain. Two highly educated, anguished siblings, needlessly berated me even after selling their deceased father's house in one week, and sent malevolent emails and text messages to me for no reason. Realize that sometimes the death of a parent can bring out the worst in people, so never take it personally.

The last two stories I will share involve short sale homes; a selling phenomenon that once dominated the housing market. Two of my clients needed to sell their properties, because their mortgages exceeded the value of their homes, and both shared several other commonalities. Each of these nice men went through a heart-wrenching divorce, each once worked full-time in the construction industry, and each lost much of their business.

The first home sale proved to be the most challenging after my client (an unemployed general contractor in failing health), in his distressed state, decided to take a shotgun and chase after his teenage son only to have the police and SWAT team arrive and surround his home (with my real estate sign in prominent position), much to the chagrin of on-looking neighbors and media. Sadly, the dad went to jail, and their family unit deteriorated completely. Miraculously, a real estate investor later purchased his home and did a beautiful job of restoring it.

In my other short sale listing, my owner truly endured more than one should have to handle. My client lost his first house due to divorce, lost a home he acquired as a bachelor, and then lost the home he purchased for his mother. He also lost his dog to old age and, sadly, didn't even know. It was only when the lender employed an appraiser and found the sickly dog's remains lying in the basement that I was informed about the situation. Needless to say, animal remains become toxic over time, and the resulting remediation required special suits and masks.

While these two listings appear extreme, the reality seems clear: it can happen to anyone. The stress of a home sale doesn't just happen to sellers; real estate agents also feel the stress of overcoming immense hurdles on the road to a sale.

In Praise of REALTORS®

Who hasn't heard builders say that real estate agents will say and do anything to get a sale, while consumers will cry about how builders can be so dishonest? While this kind of discord exists with unprofessional and unethical people in real estate, generally speaking, we as a group of professionals practice our craft ethically and responsibly. In fact, we need to stop belittling ourselves and remind the public of the tremendous value a REALTOR® (a member of the National Association of REALTORS®) and anyone in the housing industry brings to the economy. If we are remiss in casting a positive light on our profession, those of us in real estate will continue to rank nearly last in surveys that grade different professions. Let me remind everyone what William D. North wrote in the 1978 edition of The Executive Officer, "A history of rampant land speculation, exploitation, and disorder" reined until the 1913 Code of Ethics of the National Association of REALTORS® was adopted. "REALTORS® were the first business group outside the 'learned professions of medicine, engineering, and law' to adopt a Code of Ethics." The National Association of REALTORS® requires REALTORS® to attend a Code of Ethics and Standards of Practice class every two years in order to perpetuate our long history of professionalism.

So many REALTORS® possess great salesmanship, but in a declining market, some REALTORS® can become much more ruthless in their pursuit of a listing than even they would think possible. Additionally, many agents often forget that a person's word and handshake means something while waiting to seal the deal with pen and paper. While it is not for me to judge another agent's actions, having never walked in their shoes, some agent's pursuit of new listings often borders on misconduct. But one thing must be remembered; for some agents, making a sale often means the difference between paying the mortgage and putting food on the table. While every agent conducts his or her own business in a different way, there remains one area that some listing agents take advantage of during a declining market. It isn't uncommon for a listing agent to overprice a home's value (whether on purpose or by mistake) in order to get a listing. We all know a home's value stems from marketplace facts and comparable sales that cannot be controlled. In addition, the Code of Ethics clearly states that no REALTOR® "shall deliberately mislead the owner as to market value in attempting to secure a listing." Some will argue that this practice rarely occurs, and since I don't possess any related statistics, I will leave it at that.

Now you know the truth about the many difficulties a professional REALTOR® experiences. Happily, I survived, and my stories prove it! Many of my proudest moments occurred when upholding the values and ethics of a REALTOR®.

13

Beyond the Role of Listing and Selling Agent

In new construction a sales agent is selling both a builder's reputation and a new home. In the resale market an agent needs to sell their reputation as a sales person, the real estate company's reputation and sales tools, and a used home. A builder never needs to consider how his client lives; a listing agent, on the other hand, gets to know every inch of a client's home and spends a lot of time getting to know him or her. It's quite commonplace to make lasting friendships with past clients and to find yourself in a much more supportive, encouraging role in order to get all parties to agree upon a price and closing date.

Know Before You Go

The 1980's "Golden Age" of subdivision building glorified an old adage, "if you build it, they will come." Today, sellers, real estate professionals, builders and re-modelers need to understand that, in many areas of the country, the selling and re-modeling of homes, especially in urban, mixed-use, and spot lot building, continue to substantially replace large, expansive suburban neighborhoods. With the Great

Recession behind us and consumers now willing to purchase homes, many in the industry have adopted a new adage for the Technology Era: "Know before you go." Whether reselling a home, purchasing a piece of land to build upon or remodeling a home to flip, it's always a good idea to conduct a market study. This will help confirm the location, price, average length of time on market (absorption rate) and style of homes that appeal most to potential buyers in the area. The housing industry remains market-driven, not market-driving. Home buyers and their expectations, preferences, and finances continue to be the primary consideration for determining what type of home they will most likely want to buy.

Because the buyers' desires and preferences remain so vital to the sale of homes, the National Association of REALTORS® and National Association of Home Builders frequently conduct market studies. These studies help determine what types of homes should be built and what should satisfy the home buying public's requirements for housing. For example, recent studies show that divorce rates rose after the Great Recession, causing a rise in housing needs for single parents. Student debt continues to weigh down first-time homebuyers, but it doesn't have to keep them from buying; it just means that they have to buy something less expensive. Retiring homeowners still want to down-size. Blended families, especially with aging parents, often require very specific housing needs, as do international buyers.

In the 1980's, not only did the majority of homebuyers prefer to place their housing investments in suburban areas, but they also wanted better everything. Today, the size of homes, as well as what is considered to be "standard" features in housing, continues to evolve. For example, a master bathroom with a large jetted tub is less popular than a large, double-sized walk-in shower with jets everywhere. Double sliding shower doors now appear old-fashioned compared to an attractive, frameless glass wall or door. Old is new again as reclaimed wood and designs from the past become more appealing. Energy-efficiency remains an important component of a home, and a kitchen for gathering remains its heart.

Many of today's buyers still expect to own more than one home in their lifetime. As financial circumstances improve and lifestyles change, so do buyers' needs and desires, creating a "move up" market in housing and raising the question, what will future generations expect when it comes time to buy a home? Those who still aspire to be in a comfortable, modern home on a large lot in the suburbs or semi-rural areas must also recognize how important it remains to continue to preserve our farmland, open space, and environmentally sensitive areas.

Land and water is a limited commodity, and so we must cherish them. Remember, there is no new water; what water we have just regenerates itself. The same is true with land; there is a finite amount of our earth in which to build. Population growth, economic stability, available and affordable housing, and land preservation seem to be objectives mutually attainable only with the cooperation of the various interests, working toward solutions that ensure sustainable growth for current generations and those to come. A balance must be struck between competing issues and concerns.

Real estate professionals, builders, remodelers and investors continue to explore all available alternatives for housing. These alternatives include higher density communities with smaller home sites and more areas of common open space, and the utilizing of "in-fill land" in existing areas to build fewer homes instead of creating new, larger communities. Developers continue to seek the development of "brown fields" through the cleanup and remediation of previously contaminated ground and revitalizing older suburban and urban areas to create new opportunities and locations for home ownership.

Builders, remodelers, and investors recognize that issues and concerns over growth may well change the future of home building, including what, where and how we build. Likewise, the home buying public must also rethink its expectations for housing if we want to work together to provide for economic growth and housing opportunities for future generations.

If it's possible to remember only one important concept from this book, I urge remembering this. It would be wise to re-invest in a home while living in it so that when it has to be sold, it can sell! By remodeling a home in stages, it will keep it from looking completely old and ugly. So, if possible, wait a few years between every major remodeling project—this will ensure a lot more people will like the home.

For those who want to be a real estate agent, here's the reality of the industry. It's really not particularly difficult to become a real estate salesperson. Yes, it requires class time, study time and the ability to pass the test to get your license. It's the one profession (aside from a car salesperson) that appeals to so many because they mistakenly think owning a home qualifies them to be an expert. Guess again!

When ready to sell a home, it's not always easy to find a professional, knowledgeable real estate agent. In fact, it can be downright scary!

🏠 🏠 🏠 🏠 🏠 🏠

It is my intention to empower everyone to work towards selling a house for more money and in less time. Have fun getting the home and marketing materials ready to go, because then it's possible to step back and enjoy the ride! As stated from the very beginning, it's the house that sells the house. No one can talk someone into buying a house, if it's not the place to call home. Remember this adage: if wanting top dollar for a home, it has to look top dollar!

And finally, let's talk about the stresses and strains of selling a home. It's OK. It is difficult and overwhelming and asking for help is not a sign of weakness. Life is too short—go make some memorable moments SELLING UP!

Notes

www.ingramcontent.com/pod-product-compliance
Lightning Source LLC
Chambersburg PA
CBHW072112280526
45788CB00006B/2499